SMITH WIGGLESWORTH

SMITH WIGGLESWORTH
THE COMPLETE STORY

Julian Wilson

Authentic

25 24 23 22 21 20 19 7 6 5 4 3 2 1

First published 2002 by Authentic Publishing

Second edition first published 2011 by
Authentic Media Limited, reprinted 2012, 2017

This third edition first published 2019 by
Authentic Media Limited,
PO Box 6326, Bletchley, Milton Keynes, MK1 9GG
www.authenticmedia.co.uk

ISBN: 978-1-78893-102-1
978-1-78893-103-8 (ebook)

British Library Cataloguing in Publication Data
A catalogue record for this book is available from the British Library

Cover design by Arnel Gregorio
arrowdesigns01@gmail.com

Printed and bound by CPI Group (UK) Ltd, Croydon, CR0 7YY

CONTENTS

Dedication   vii
Acknowledgements   ix
Foreword   xi
Introduction   xiii

1. The Early Years   1
2. Polly   14
3. Bradford and the Bowland Street Mission   21
4. Baptised by Fire   38
5. First America, Then the World   59
6. Wigglesworth the Man   69
7. Only Believe   94
8. Signs, Wonders and Miracles   109
9. Opposition and Criticism   129
10. Campaigns of the 1920s   144
11. Triumphing Over Trials   179
12. And Then He Was Not; for God Took Him   194

Epilogue: The Wigglesworth Legacy   205
Endnotes   207
Bibliography   212

Dedicated to the two women in my life –
Xiao-Wen and Lian

ACKNOWLEDGEMENTS

Biographers, more often than not, owe a debt of gratitude to those who have gone before them, and in this respect, I am no exception. Of particular note is Stanley Frodsham's *Smith Wigglesworth, Apostle of Faith*, the first biography of Wigglesworth, which features Wigglesworth's own account of his life and the recollections of his daughter and son-in-law, James Salter. Other biographies of merit are Jack Hywel-Davies' *Baptised by Fire*; Desmond Cartwright's recently published biography, *The Real Smith Wigglesworth*; and *Seven Pentecostal Pioneers* by Colin Whittaker, which contains a chapter on Wigglesworth. Providing excellent background material on Wigglesworth and the Pentecostal movement are Donald Gee's classic, *The Pentecostal Movement*; J.E. Worsfold's *A History of the Charismatic Movement in New Zealand*; *New Zealand's Greatest Revival* by Harry V. Roberts; Barry Chant's history of the Australian Pentecostal movement, *Heart of Fire*; and David du Plessis' autobiography, *A Man Called Mr Pentecost*. Also of significant value are the reminiscences of three individuals who knew Wigglesworth well: Albert Hibbert, William Hacking and George Stormont.

Roberts Liardon deserves recognition for his diligence in compiling and publishing a number of volumes of Wigglesworth's sermons and teachings, including the definitive *Smith Wigglesworth: The Complete Collection of His Life Teachings*. A special mention must be made of the Donald Gee Centre for Pentecostal and Charismatic Research, which houses a full complement of the Assemblies of God publication, *Redemption Tidings*, copies of *Confidence*, the *Elim Evangel* and other priceless source material. Thanks also to LeSea Ministries for granting me permission to quote from *I Saw the Glory & My Relationship with Smith Wigglesworth*, featuring Lester Sumrall's reminiscences of Wigglesworth.

I would like to express my gratitude, in particular, to the following for their generous and selfless responses to my appeals for assistance: Dr Dave Garrard, archivist of the Donald Gee Centre for Pentecostal and Charismatic Research, Dr Dave Allen of Mattersey College, Brett Knowles of the University of Otago in New Zealand, Pastor Mike Knott and Fipi Vatucicila of Elim International Christian Church in Wellington, New Zealand, Pastor Roberts Liardon and Laurel Peters and Erica Cimaglia of Roberts Liardon Ministries, Dr Trevor Hutley, Wayne Warner, director of the archives of the Assemblies of God Flower Pentecostal Heritage Center, the late William Hacking and Desmond Cartwright.

Finally, a very special thank you to Dr Jack Hywel-Davies for his help with the book and for his thought-provoking and insightful foreword.

FOREWORD

Smith Wigglesworth was not a popular man. Although I first came to know him more than sixty years ago and had personal contact with him on several occasions during that time, I did not find him an attractive personality. He was gruff, rarely smiling and somewhat austere. I didn't find it easy to talk to him, but then I was only eighteen at the time and an insignificant student, albeit head student of Howard Carter's Bible School. That was when I first saw him 'in action' and I must confess it made a significant impression on me. Though he had an abrupt, unpolished manner, I recognised a kind of 'presence' about him. However, although I was frequently asked to 'look after' world-renowned Pentecostal personalities who came to the school's weekly convention meetings at Zion College, a prestigious baronial-style hall alongside the River Thames in the City of London, he was the least friendly man to receive my attention.

Thinking of Wigglesworth and his idiosyncrasies, I came across these comments, by chance, on the prophet Samuel's search for a new king for Israel. The sons of Jesse, a well-known farmer, were all paraded before the elderly prophet as a suitable king. They were fine looking officers in King Saul's army. But God told the prophet that they were not his choice. So Samuel asked Jesse if he had another son. The old man said, 'Yes, he's out minding the sheep.' He was David, who was just a lad. So David was brought before Samuel and God said, 'This is the one, anoint him.' God said to Samuel, 'Don't judge by his appearance or height . . . The LORD doesn't make decisions the way you do!' (1 Samuel 16:7 NLT). And the comments? God was to choose David, who would have made a good minister of music if he had had better morals. He also chose Moses who stuttered and lost his temper. Elijah was chosen even though he was a man of depression. And John the Baptist lacked tact and dressed like a hippie. God looked on them not as they were but as what they could do in his service. I thought how true that was of dear Wigglesworth: an illiterate, inarticulate, uneducated man.

As you read this most detailed and frank account of Smith Wigglesworth's life by Julian Wilson, I recommend that you think of the outstanding, even unique ways in which he carried out God's instructions. He was called the 'Apostle of Faith' and you had to have a lot of faith to confront him. He could be frightening, but he was miraculously effective. When God called him 'home', God broke the mould. As I once counselled a New York pastor who asked me, 'How can I be like Wigglesworth?' – do not try. Take inspiration from his life, don't dwell on his peculiarities and weaknesses and just allow God to take you as you are.

Jack Hywel-Davies

INTRODUCTION

In the two thousand years since the birth of Christianity, few individuals have made such an impact on the world for the gospel as the Yorkshire-born plumber turned evangelist, Smith Wigglesworth. Multitudes were saved worldwide as he ministered, and miracles of healing and deliverance occurred that have rarely been witnessed since the days of the apostles. As Barry Chant has commented: 'It can safely be said that no one has ever had a ministry quite like his.'

Wigglesworth's life began inauspiciously, with little hint of what was to come. Born into abject poverty in rural Victorian Britain, and compelled, from the age of seven, to work in a woollen mill to help support his family, Wigglesworth was denied an education and was illiterate until his mid-twenties, when he was taught to read and write by his wife Polly. A poor speaker, who stammered and stumbled in the pulpit, his preaching ministry only began at the relatively advanced age of forty-eight, following his baptism by the Holy Spirit. From then on, for the next forty years, he preached powerfully on platforms across the globe, although to much larger assemblies abroad than in his home country.

In his early years, Wigglesworth struggled vainly to contain his explosive temper, a weakness exacerbated by two years spent in the spiritual wilderness. Following what he described as his sanctification, he became, according to one who knew him well, the purest, most Christ-like person he had ever known. However, he remained throughout his life blunt and tactless – at all times totally himself. This outspokenness led some to believe that he was hard and unapproachable, but his gruff, brusque exterior concealed a heart overflowing with compassion. He would often be observed weeping over a deformed baby or those ravaged by disease. His life was one of non-stop ministry and it was rare for him to return home, according to his son-in-law, James Salter, 'but that he had led someone to the Lord or ministered healing to a needy person'.

There were two things that made Smith Wigglesworth exceptional: a level of communion with God that few ever achieve in their lifetime, and unquestioning faith and trust in the Bible. In his latter years, Wigglesworth was in continual, unbroken fellowship with his Lord, seldom allowing half an hour to pass without prayer. His passion for the Scriptures was insatiable and he claimed to have read only the Bible from the time he learned to read to his death at the age of nearly eighty-eight. Emanating from his intimacy with God and His Word was a divine power rarely equalled, and such was the anointing that rested on Wigglesworth that his mere presence could convict those with whom he came into contact of their sin. Many who visited him at Victor Road in Bradford described the sense of awe they experienced as they became aware of the presence of God in his home, remarking that it was like stepping on holy ground.

Unmoved by circumstances, adversity or the condemnation of man, Wigglesworth fearlessly proclaimed the gospel, prayed for the sick and cast out demons; his natural boldness magnified by the Holy Spirit. Unique among ministers, before or since, he would often, controversially, strike the part of the body of the sufferer that was afflicted, claiming that as virtually all disease was satanic in origin that he was not hitting the person but the devil. Many accused Wigglesworth of being needlessly harsh and insensitive, but could not argue with the dramatic results of his unorthodox methods of ministry.

How do those who claim that divine healing ceased at the end of the first century AD with the close of the Apostolic Age, explain a phenomenon like Smith Wigglesworth? Astounding miracles, many officially documented and observed by hundreds, occurred as he prayed, including cancerous tumours that literally dropped off sufferers, ear drums that were created, eyes that received sight, the paralysed able to walk and the dead raised to life. Wigglesworth's life demonstrates the potential of an individual wholly consecrated to God, who has an unshakeable faith in His Word. It also begs the question: would those who received salvation, healing and deliverance have done so had they not come into contact with Smith Wigglesworth?

It is fascinating to reflect on how Wigglesworth would be perceived today in this politically correct and litigious age: as a faith healer, charlatan or just plain eccentric? Would he, like John Wesley, fan the flames of revival in his homeland, resulting in a return of the masses to genuine Christianity or be marginalised as a fanatical fundamentalist? He would, undoubtedly, be forced to endure intense and sceptical media scrutiny and the intrusive glare of the television cameras. It is possible that the assemblies at which he preached would prohibit him from striking people when he prayed for them. Such a physical approach to ministry would now result, almost certainly, at least in the Western world, in multiple lawsuits and possible arrest and prosecution for assault.

It is doubtful whether Smith Wigglesworth would be
perturbed at the hostility and cynicism of the world or
that he would change his style. He was, and remained to
the end of his life, a blunt, working-class Yorkshireman of
indomitable faith, whose signature exhortation resonates
as powerfully today as it did in his lifetime, 'Only believe,
only believe. All things are possible, only believe.'

Chapter One

THE EARLY YEARS

Yorkshire, England, 12 March 1947. A car is moving slowly across a harsh, white-blanketed landscape. It is the worst winter in living memory, and flurries of powdery snow beat against the windscreen before being flicked away by the whirring windscreen-wipers. Sitting in the back seat in a heavy black overcoat, thick woollen scarf and flat cloth cap is an old, white-haired man with a full moustache, the tip of his nose turned crimson by the cold. Smith Wigglesworth is being driven to the funeral of his friend and fellow minister, Wilfred Richardson, at Glad Tidings Hall in the city of Wakefield. The car comes to a halt outside the imposing neo-Gothic edifice and the driver gets out and opens the rear passenger door. Wigglesworth eases himself out of his seat slowly and stiffly, and then proceeds to mount the steps of the church. He is greeted warmly by a man at the entrance, the muffled strains of a hymn being played on a pipe organ escaping from the half-open door. As he walks with measured steps, back ramrod straight, down the centre aisle and then scales the steps leading to the vestry, people sitting on the wooden pews turn to catch a fleeting glimpse of the revered figure and whisper to each other in awed, hushed tones.

Among those warming themselves in front of an open coal fire in the vestry while waiting for the service to begin are James Salter, Wigglesworth's son-in-law, the renowned evangelist and Bible teacher, Donald Gee, Frederick Watson, a member of the Executive Council of the Assemblies of God and the church secretary, Elder Hibbert, whose daughter Wigglesworth had prayed for a week earlier. Wigglesworth removes his cap and greets his fellow ministers in his usual fashion – with a gentle smile, a few encouraging words and a kiss of Christian love. After embracing Hibbert, he enquires impatiently about his daughter, his eyes bright with anticipation for what he expects to be an account of her divine healing.

As Hibbert lowers his gaze and replies hesitatingly, that she is a little better, Wigglesworth heaves a deep, body convulsing sigh of disappointment, his head drops down onto his chest and he slumps forward into the startled church secretary's arms. The others react involuntarily to support the limp Wigglesworth as Hibbert staggers under his weight, gently lowering his inert form to the vestry floor. James Salter checks his pulse and then his heart, and slowly shakes his bowed head with an air of grim finality. Grief-stricken groans mingle with frantic cries of, 'Lord, raise him up!' as they stare transfixed at the body, eyes filled suddenly with hot tears, barely able to comprehend that the great evangelist, whom many believed would not experience death, was truly dead.

November 1865. Six-year-old Smith Wigglesworth is grubbing up turnips in a field, the tops of which have been eaten by livestock, his little hands cracked and chapped by the biting winter cold. It starts to rain and Smith looks up at the dark, brooding sky in despair, as rivulets of water stream down his upturned face. The working day over, he trudges, chilled to the bone and desperately tired, back to the family home, a bleak, two-room stone cottage. In the darkened, draught-ridden interior, the gloom pierced only by the light of a log fire, the family – John and Martha Wigglesworth and their three sons and a daughter – sit huddled for warmth around the hearth, eating a simple dinner of fatty bacon, potatoes and bread, washed down with copious quantities of weak tea.

Smith Wigglesworth was born on 10 June 1859 in the West Yorkshire village of Menston on the edge of Ilkley Moor, approximately seven miles from the heart of the industrial town of Bradford. His father, John Wigglesworth, was an agricultural labourer, and regular work was never certain in an age when there was no job security, and employment was often on a day-to-day basis. His mother, Martha, eked out her husband's meagre wage as best she could and made the family's clothes from old garments given to her by friends and relatives.

One day in the middle of winter, Smith's father picked up some work digging a large ditch for three shillings and sixpence. Martha suggested he wait for a while for the ground to thaw to make his task easier. But the family had neither money nor food and John Wigglesworth was obliged to hack away at the frozen ground with a pickaxe. After digging more than a yard down, he was beginning to lose heart when he struck some soft, wet clay. As he hurled up a clod, a robin suddenly appeared and snatched a worm from the freshly turned ground and ate it. The robin then flew off to a nearby tree and proceeded to sing contentedly. So entranced was John Wigglesworth by the little bird's exuberance that he attacked the ground with new vigour, saying to himself, 'If that robin can sing like that for a worm, surely I can work like a father for my good wife and my four fine children!'

John Wigglesworth was a nature lover and the small cottage was always filled with cages containing a menagerie of songbirds. Smith inherited his father's passion for the countryside. Recalled Wigglesworth years later: 'Like my father, I had a great love for birds and at every opportunity I would be out looking for their nests. I always knew where there were some eighty or ninety of them. One time I found a nest full of fledglings and, thinking they were abandoned, I adopted them, taking them home and making a place for them in my bedroom. Somehow the parent birds discovered them and would fly in through the open window and feed their young ones. One time I had a thrush and a lark feeding their young ones in my room. My brothers and I would catch some songbirds by means of bird-lime, bring them home and later sell them in the market.'

When Smith was seven years old, his father found work as a weaver in one of the numerous woollen mills in Bradford, the centre of the worsted cloth-making industry in Britain. John Wigglesworth was also able to secure employment for Smith – his second job to date – and his elder brother, thus depriving both of anything more than a rudimentary education.

Six days a week, Smith crawled shivering from his bed at five o'clock, snatched a quick breakfast, before setting off for the two-mile hike to the mill, huddled in his old hand-me-down overcoat with sleeves three inches too long, to be there by six. Often he would complain wearily to his father after another twelve-hour day working in the stifling heat and cloying dust of the mill, 'It's a long time from six while six in t'mill.' His father would reply softly with tears of regret in his eyes, 'Well six o'clock will always come, my son.'

One morning as he walked to work, a great thunderstorm erupted. In the midst of deafening claps of thunder and bolts of lighting illuminating the sky, he cried out helplessly for God's protection and became aware of being surrounded by an all-enveloping presence. He continued on his way to work with the storm still raging, soaked to the skin, but confident in the knowledge that he would come to no harm.

From an early age, Wigglesworth had a yearning to know God. 'I can never recollect a time when I did not long for God,' he once remarked to his friend and biographer, Stanley Frodsham. 'Even though neither Father nor Mother knew God, I was always seeking Him. I would often kneel down in the field and ask Him to help me. I would ask Him especially to enable me to find where the birds' nests were, and after I had prayed I seemed to have an instinct to know exactly where to look.' Years later, Wigglesworth recalled how he would lie down in a field and praise God, 'until heaven seemed to be let down, till it seemed like glory.'[1]

Smith's grandmother, Bella – a Wesleyan Methodist born in 1778, who lived possibly into her nineties, and who may have heard John Wesley preach when he visited Bradford – took him along to meetings at the little Methodist chapel in the village which was built in 1826. At one early Sunday morning revival meeting, the congregation sang and clapped their hands in worship as they danced round an old combustion stove in the centre of the chapel.

One can imagine the eight-year-old Smith staring in wonder at the scene and starting, perhaps shyly and tentatively at first, to join in himself. 'As I clapped my hands and sang with them,' recalled Wigglesworth, 'a clear knowledge of the new birth came into my soul. I looked to the Lamb of Calvary. I believed that He loved me and died for me. Life came in – eternal life – and I knew that I had received a new life that had come from God. I was born again. I saw God wants us so badly that he has made the condition as simple as He possibly could – "Only believe." That experience was real and I have never doubted my salvation since that day.'

From that day on, Wigglesworth became a soul-winner. The first soul he won for Christ was his mother (and later he won his father, although Wigglesworth was to lament while preaching in California in 1922 that despite being convicted of their sin many times, his two brothers were still unsaved). Unfortunately, like his mother, Smith's speech was unintelligible and he struggled vainly to express his thoughts with his limited vocabulary. He loved to listen to the testimonies of those in the chapel in Menston on a Sunday, but when he rose self-consciously to give his own, he would stumble tongue-tied through one half-finished sentence after another, before bursting into tears of frustration and embarrassment. Seeing his distress one Sunday, three old men in the congregation who knew him well felt moved to lay hands on the disconsolate Smith and pray for him. As they did so, the Holy Spirit touched him and he discovered to his joy that he could speak more clearly, although still only to individuals and small gatherings. Public speaking would remain, for years to come, a tortuous, nerve-racking experience.

Although John Wigglesworth was not a member of the Church of England, and rarely attended services at the parish church where Smith had been baptised as a baby, he was friendly with the curate, with whom he often shared a pint of ale at the local coaching inn, and was eager for his sons to be involved in church life. Thus it was that Smith and one of his brothers found themselves in the church choir, and Wigglesworth, with his sharp mind, quickly learnt the hymns and chants off by heart, despite his virtual illiteracy. Indeed, he made such an impression that he was selected for confirmation by the bishop and full membership of the church.

It turned out, unexpectedly, to be a profound spiritual experience. 'I can remember,' recalled Wigglesworth, 'as he [the bishop] imposed his hands on me I had a similar experience to the one I had forty years later when I was baptised in the Holy Spirit. My whole body was filled with a consciousness of God's presence, a consciousness that remained with me for days.' After the confirmation service, in the vestry, while Smith stood alone pondering his extraordinary encounter with God, he observed the other boys engaging in raucous horseplay and wondered why he was different.

In 1872, when Smith Wigglesworth was thirteen, the family moved to Bradford to be closer to the woollen mills, which, with their tall chimneys belching smoke, characterised the rapidly burgeoning town (Bradford was not designated a city until 1897). Smith found employment in another mill where he was assigned to assist one of the mill's steam fitters, who was a godly man and a member of the Plymouth Brethren. As well as teaching Wigglesworth the fundamentals of plumbing, he gave the young convert a solid foundation in Bible doctrine, including believers' baptism by full immersion – Smith was baptised for the second time when he was seventeen – and the Second Coming of Christ. Time and again, when Smith felt that he had failed God in some way, he would run to work, heart pounding, and heave a sigh of relief when he saw his friend, realising that the Lord had not come in the night and left him behind.

Burning with evangelistic fervour and seldom to be seen without his little New Testament, even though he could only read a few words, Wigglesworth was soon sharing his faith with the men and boys at the mill. This often led to rejection and ridicule, reactions that were always a mystery to Smith, although he was to admit years later that his bluntness and lack of tact – traits that had already become obvious – were partly to blame for the rebuffs.

Despite his confirmation as a member of the Church of England, Wigglesworth elected to attend a Methodist church when he arrived in Bradford, attracted by the congregation's passion for missions. But then, in 1875, William Booth, founder of the Salvation Army, visited Bradford and held a series of evangelistic meetings that resulted in the establishing of a presence in the town. These early Salvationists impressed Wigglesworth immensely with their zeal for winning souls and, after attending a few meetings, he decided to throw himself wholeheartedly into their work, although he never became a member of the Salvation Army. 'We would have all nights [sic] of prayer,' recalled Wigglesworth. 'Many would be prostrated under the power of the Spirit, sometimes for as long as twenty-four hours at a time. We called that the baptism in the Spirit in those days. We would join together and claim in faith fifty or a hundred souls every week and know that we would get them . . . The power of God rested upon the worst characters and they were saved. It reached every class. Drunkards were saved right and left and the next day when they were put up for testimony their testimony thrilled the place so that the power of God fell upon others who in turn became witnesses to the salvation of Christ. There was no such building large enough to hold the work. The meetings were in open marketplaces and they put big wagons there for platforms. The people who were saved the night before would speak and the power of God would fall.'

When he was eighteen, Wigglesworth, by now well versed in the art of plumbing, left the mill to seek employment as a plumber, and decided to approach the boss of one of Bradford's most renowned plumbing firms. Immaculately dressed in a suit, sparkling white stiff collar, and shoes polished to a brilliant shine, he marched boldly up to the boss's house and knocked firmly on the front door, fiddling with his tie and clearing his throat nervously while waiting for the door to open. After explaining himself to the gruff Yorkshireman standing in the doorway eyeing him suspiciously, his hopes appeared to be dashed. 'No, I don't need anyone,' came the terse reply in flat Yorkshire tones. Fortunately, Wigglesworth had the presence of mind to be more diplomatic than usual and replied politely, 'Thank you, sir, I'm sorry.'

As he headed, disappointed, back down the path to the front gate, the plumber watched him leave with a growing sense of unease. After a moment's hesitation he strode quickly to the front door and called Wigglesworth back. 'There's something about you that's different. I just can't let you go,' said the plumber somewhat perplexed, and offered the delighted Wigglesworth a job. His first assignment was to fit a row of houses with water pipes, which he completed in a week. When he announced that he had finished the job, his boss was astonished. 'It can't possibly be done!' he replied, assuming shoddy workmanship and peering sceptically at Wigglesworth. Yet, when he examined the work he found that it was perfect. Such was Wigglesworth's prodigious work-rate that for the next two years the plumber struggled to keep him fully employed.

While his career progressed and his involvement with the Salvation Army led to a deepening of his spiritual life, Wigglesworth paid close attention to his fitness, being a firm believer in keeping the body, the temple of the Lord, in good condition. A keen sportsman who enjoyed a game of cricket and bowls, Wigglesworth, when time permitted, would mount his bicycle and head off for the

Yorkshire Dales, indulging his child-like fascination with nature, marvelling at the craggy ravines, crystal clear waterfalls and lush moorland covered in a profusion of wild flowers. But even while relaxing, young Smith's thoughts were never far from the souls of men and women. On one ten-day cycle tour accompanied by a friend, numerous stops along the way were made to witness to passers-by, resulting in, on average, three salvations a day.

In 1879, hearing of the myriad of opportunities for ambitious young men in the booming port city of Liverpool, Smith gave in his notice, bade an emotional farewell to his family and friends and crossed the Pennine hills into the county of Lancashire which, in those days of limited travel, might as well have been a foreign land.

Armed with considerable experience and excellent references, Wigglesworth quickly found employment as a plumber and settled into life in his new home. Liverpool was, by the 1870s, one of Britain's major ports, second only to London in terms of volume of trade, and was the main distribution centre for many of the goods manufactured in the industrial heartland of the North of England. The city also had strong commercial links with the port cities of the American Eastern Seaboard, including New York, Boston, Philadelphia and Baltimore, from which tall-masted clippers crossed the Atlantic, laden with raw cotton and tobacco.

Yet, beyond Liverpool's bustling docks and shipyards, and its majestic civic buildings, lay poverty unparalleled anywhere in the country. Tens of thousands were crammed into closed courts of tightly-packed tenements that had no running water and often only one 'privy' or just open cesspools serving the entire court. This resulted in conditions of indescribable filth and squalor. Such living conditions proved perfect breeding grounds for cholera, typhus and smallpox, outbreaks of which raged periodically throughout the nineteenth century, as well as other diseases such as tuberculosis and dysentery. In 1870, Liverpool had both the highest population density – 66,000 per square mile – and the highest mortality rate of any city in Britain. A third of all babies born in Liverpool died during their first year, and average life expectancy in the worst districts was a mere fifteen years.

A report in the Salvation Army's *The War Cry* in August 1880 described the conditions graphically:

Those who have not been cannot imagine the depths of sin in this, one of the most important cities in England. And last Sunday, being the anniversary, we made a special attack upon the enemy's camp, when we had Captain Taylor, ADC, with us; also Captain Richardson and Lieutenant Butts who have arrived to take command with us. Commencing at seven, the soldiers met to be supplied with ammunition and again at ten we met and marched through some of the very worst streets in the town, and to stand and meet the sin by which we were surrounded was enough to make our hearts bleed. There were the women with bare feet, black, bloated faces, and their long hair hanging in wild disorder down their backs and covered with rags called dresses but a disgrace to the name. Children running about quite nude and others almost so. Men of all climes and countries, lounging about smoking, laughing and jeering or throwing stones and mud. Everywhere and everything seemed to have the appearance of wretchedness and misery.[2]

Wigglesworth was no stranger to poverty, but as he walked the stinking streets and alleys of Liverpool's slums, he was horrified by the conditions in which this seething mass of humanity was forced to exist. But what tore at his heart most and brought tears to his eyes were the children, many of whom were destitute, spending their days rummaging through piles of garbage for scraps of food. Others, as young as five, lay slumped in doorways, blind drunk on gin, while young prostitutes, barely into their teens, clad in gaudy silk dresses, their cheeks heavily rouged, paraded the pavements in search of customers.

In his anguish, Wigglesworth, who joined with the Salvation Army's newly founded Liverpool corps, determined grimly that he had to take action. Each week, he tramped through the city's vilest districts inviting children to a shed by the docks provided by his employer who admired his fervour. Like some latter-day Pied Piper he would lead scores of them, ragged and barefoot, through the streets, as passers-by gaped in astonishment, to the shed where he gave them food paid for out of his own wages. Once they had had their fill, Wigglesworth explained, simply and tenderly, God's plan of salvation. And many of the children, who had never experienced human love in their young lives, came to know the love of Christ.

But his all-consuming passion to see the lost saved drove him to do more. He visited hospital wards and ministered to the sick and dying, and boarded ships in the dockyards from every corner of the globe to testify boldly of his Lord to the tough, weather-beaten sailors who gathered on deck to listen in rapt attention to the young Yorkshire plumber. Recalled Wigglesworth of his days in Liverpool, the memories of which he was to describe as among his most precious: 'God gave me a great heart for the poor. I used to work hard and spend all I had on the poor and have nothing for myself. I fasted all day every Sunday and prayed, and I never remember seeing less than fifty souls saved by the power of God in the meetings with the children, in the hospitals, on the ships and in the Salvation Army.'

Recognising the loving and compassionate heart that beat beneath Wigglesworth's gruff, granite-like exterior, the commanding officer of the Liverpool corps would often invite him to speak at Salvation Army meetings: requests that always puzzled Smith, for preaching from the pulpit was still an agonising ordeal. Reluctantly he agreed, but inevitably he would falter in mid-sentence, as he searched desperately for the words to express his thoughts, before grinding to a halt, broken and weeping. But as the tears coursed down his cheeks an extraordinary thing would happen: men and women across the hall – many of them the dregs of society – would rise from their seats and come to the altar on bended knee, heads bowed, as they confessed their sins and made the Saviour their own.

Three years had now passed since Smith Wigglesworth had arrived in Liverpool, and his compassion for the lost burned with a greater intensity than ever. But now he sensed the call of God to return to Bradford to be reunited with the young Salvation Army lieutenant whom he had met before he left his native Yorkshire: the woman he was often to describe affectionately as 'the best girl in the world'.

Chapter Two

POLLY

One night in 1877, a large crowd gathered in the cobbled square of Bradford's ancient market place. Their curiosity had been aroused by members of a new religious movement known as the Christian Mission – soon to be renamed the Salvation Army – who were singing what appeared to be jaunty music-hall songs with great gusto, accompanied by a brass ensemble and the resonating thud of a big bass drum. As the strains of 'Bless His Name, He Sets Me Free' (to the tune of the popular ditty 'Champagne Charlie is My Name') dwindled, Tillie 'Gypsy' Smith, a young, swarthy-skinned girl with dark bright eyes, stepped onto a wooden box and opened her Bible.

'There is salvation,' came her impassioned cry, 'for all who will stop and think and look to Christ as their personal Saviour.' Her opening remarks were met by a volley of jeers and oaths from hostile elements in the crowd. Suddenly a rotten egg whizzed through the air and struck the girl on the side of the face, the greenish-yellow yoke trickling down her cheek. Wiping away the fetid mess with a handkerchief, she continued her fiery message undaunted.

Among the throng of people that night, was another young girl of similar age who listened to Tillie's message with intense curiosity. Intrigued by the commotion, Polly had pushed her way to the front of the crowd and now gazed up at the young girl who spoke with such fiery conviction about her Lord and Saviour.

Her sermon concluded, and with an impassioned plea for sinners to make Christ their own, Tillie Smith stepped off her makeshift platform and announced that their meeting would continue at a rented theatre in one of the less salubrious districts of the city. At that, the Christian Mission's motley band struck up 'Onward Christian Soldiers' on their battered instruments and marched off into the night.

Polly followed the procession warily, at a distance through the grimy cobbled streets of back-to-back terraced houses to a run-down theatre and watched it disappear inside. She followed, then stopped at the entrance, hesitating to enter. Craning her head back, she looked up at the soot-blackened façade and gaudy billboard announcing the arrival of the next travelling theatre company. Dare she go in, for her father had warned her that such places of heathen entertainment were dens of iniquity? Yet surely, she told herself, there could be nothing wrong with attending a Christian meeting, even if it was in a theatre. Her natural inquisitiveness got the better of her and, looking around furtively to see if she had been seen, she entered the dingy, poorly-lit inner sanctum. Self-consciously, Polly mounted the steps to a row of worn, red velvet seats in the gallery, enclosed by a grimy, gold-painted balustrade that had long since lost its lustre.

Whatever reservations Polly may still have had about entering the theatre they were quickly forgotten as she listened enthralled, as new converts – among them former prostitutes, convicts, thieves and drunkards – simply and falteringly gave their heart-rending testimonies of how God had saved them from a life of hopelessness and sin. When the last had testified, Tillie Smith mounted the stage and spoke so passionately of the saving power of the Cross that Polly, gazing down from the gallery at the tiny figure pacing back and forth across the worn platform, found herself being strangely moved.

When the call finally came for sinners to repent and accept Christ as their Saviour, Polly, her eyes moist with tears, rose swiftly from her seat and made her way, with a stream of others, down the centre aisle to the foot of the platform. Weeping, she at first resisted any help as she prayed quietly. But then Tillie came and knelt beside her and together they prayed the prayer of salvation. When an assurance that her sins were forgiven flooded her being, Polly leapt to her feet, hurled her gloves in the air and cried, 'Hallelujah, it's done!'

Sitting in the audience that night in the theatre in Bradford, his eyes riveted on the radiant Polly as she gave her life to Christ, was young Smith Wigglesworth. For him it was also a momentous moment. 'It seemed as if the inspiration of God was upon her from the first,'[1] marvelled Wigglesworth as he gazed at the lovely young girl. Later, when he listened entranced as she gave her testimony, he felt that she belonged to him.

Mary Jane Featherstone, or Polly as she was known by all, came from a family of devout Methodists. Her father, a temperance lecturer, refused to accept his large inheritance built on the sale of liquor and he instilled in her the same godly principles. When Mary Jane was seventeen, her parents decided that she should acquire a trade and she was apprenticed to a milliner. But a month of cutting and stitching hats was more than enough for the high-spirited, headstrong Polly who left home for the bright lights of Bradford, where she found employment as a domestic servant in a large house.

Following her conversion, Polly made rapid progress both in her spiritual life and in the Salvation Army. Her friendship with Tillie, her brother Rodney 'Gypsy' Smith and mill worker turned evangelist, John Lawley, brought her to the attention of the Army's founder, General William Booth. Recognising her oratorical and leadership skills, Booth gave her an officer's commission, waiving the usual compulsory training.

Mary Jane was to vindicate the General's faith in her. Fearless and indomitable, she became one of the Bradford Corps' foremost soul-winners. She also had an enchanting voice, and as she sang Salvation Army songs and testified in the open air, windows of surrounding houses would be flung open and curious listeners would peer down at Polly as she sang movingly of the love of Christ for a lost world.

She and her fellow soldiers' fortitude would be tested on many occasions. As opposition to the Salvation Army intensified, it became common for soldiers to be pelted with a variety of missiles which included rotten eggs and vegetables, stones, live coals and burning sulphur, even dead rats and cats. Once Polly received a black eye from an orange that was hurled in her direction. Another cunning tactic employed by the Army's persecutors was to throw red-hot pennies into the arena at collection time expecting to hear a succession of oaths as the Salvationists seared their hands when they picked up the coins, but were disappointed by the retort of 'God bless you'.

As they both threw themselves enthusiastically into the work of the Army, attending meetings and marching through the streets of Bradford, an unlikely but intimate friendship grew between the stammering and uneducated Wigglesworth and the confident, vivacious and middle-class Polly. Wherever Polly was, there was Smith, or so it seemed, and it was not long before it became apparent to her commanding officers that they were forming a strong attachment. This contravened Salvation Army rules that forbade liaisons between officers and ordinary soldiers. Wigglesworth never actually joined the Army, which was even worse.

To pre-empt any further development of their relationship, it was decided that Polly should be transferred out of Bradford. A major was dispatched to the Army home where she was working to see whether she would be willing to start a new work in Leith on the outskirts of Edinburgh in Scotland. Polly appears to have agreed on the spot, packed her suitcase and left immediately for the railway station accompanied by the major. Wigglesworth's reaction to her abrupt departure is not recorded, but it may partly explain his decision to leave Bradford for Liverpool in 1879.

While in Leith, Polly took a particular interest in a recent convert, a young woman who lived in a grim tenement building in one of the town's slums. Her husband, a brutal, uncouth man prone to violence, fiercely opposed her attendance at Salvation Army meetings. Returning home from work early one day, he discovered Polly praying with his wife. Furious at what he considered his wife's betrayal, he threatened menacingly to forcibly eject Polly if she refused to stop praying. Terrified, his wife began to rise from her knees, when Polly grasped hold of her hand and held it tightly, reassuring the trembling woman. Shaking a little, her voice quavering and her eyes tightly shut, Polly continued to pray ignoring the increasingly violent threats. Enraged by this act of defiance, the man grabbed hold of Polly, lifted her up and carried her to the doorway, ignoring the hysterical pleas of his weeping wife to put her down.

Gripping the praying Polly firmly, the man kicked open the front door and staggered down the first of five flights of stairs. As he continued his descent, swearing profusely, his countenance one of naked fury, Polly prayed fervently with increasing desperation, 'Lord, save this man; save his soul, Lord.' With conviction tearing at his soul, the man perspiring heavily, reached the final flight of stairs. For Polly it was now or never. But then suddenly he stopped, his shoulders sagging. Polly opened her eyes to see the man sobbing, his muscular frame heaving as the tears coursed down his face, crying out for God's mercy. Gently he lowered Polly to the ground and knelt beside her, the bottom step a makeshift penitent form as she spoke softly of the cleansing blood of Jesus.

The work in Leith was flourishing and Polly was in her element, whether it was preaching in the streets or leading some slum-dweller to salvation. However, it was not long before the same thorny issue that led to her swift departure from Bradford cast a shadow over her new life: the attractive and sparkling Polly had attracted the attention of one of her Scottish fellow soldiers and in the close-knit community of the Salvation Army, rumours were rife of a relationship. Assuming the attraction was mutual, her commanding officers questioned Polly about her relationship with the soldier. When she remained tight-lipped and deflected their questions they suggested they pray, possibly in the hope that she might reveal some incriminating details. But as she led in prayer, Polly made it quite clear that she had no interest in the person concerned, concluding with, 'Lord, I do not intend to marry anyone away up here in Scotland.'

The officers brought the interview to a close, but it was not long after that Polly severed her connection with the Salvation Army. Whether the unfounded suspicions of her superior officers and the subsequent interrogation wounded her or whether she had already decided to leave the Army because of her impending marriage[2] to Wigglesworth is unclear, but in 1882, according to her daughter Alice, she resigned her commission and returned to Bradford. An alternative explanation for her sudden departure could be that she was given no choice but to leave. Salvation Army records, in a single reference to Polly, state: 'Featherstone, Mary J. (Bradford 1 1881) Code number 625 Dispo. reference 1883 p.43 Corps appointments Aberdeen II, Glasgow I, dismissed 1882.'

Another twist to the story is that Wigglesworth was to say on a number of occasions that God told him to 'come out' of the Salvation Army because, in his view, the movement 'went into natural things and the great revivals I had known in the early days ceased'. His 'coming out' coincided with Polly's departure from the Army and it is likely that, corresponding during their time apart (although he would have had to have had Polly's letters read to him and had someone write his letters because he was illiterate), they had made a joint decision to leave.

Whatever the truth of the matter, Wigglesworth gave in his notice and left Liverpool for Bradford in 1882, and that same year he and Polly were married: he was twenty-three and she was twenty-two. Their marriage was to endure for thirty years and would, in many ways, be the making of Smith Wigglesworth. Acknowledging all that he owed to his beloved wife, Wigglesworth was to say, following her death: 'I stand on this platform because of a holy woman, a woman who lived in righteousness, poured her righteousness into my life, so transforming my life from wayward indifferences of all kinds, and so shaping my life, that she was practically the means of purging me through and through.'

Chapter Three

BRADFORD AND THE BOWLAND STREET MISSION

Following her departure from the Salvation Army in 1882, Polly received many invitations from Methodist churches in Bradford and beyond to hold evangelistic meetings, and Wigglesworth encouraged her to develop her ministry, while he continued building his plumbing business. Five children – Seth, Alice, Harold, Ernest and George – were born between 1882 and 1896 and each, as would be expected, was covered in prayer. It was during the first three years of their marriage that Polly taught Smith to read and write, although, as he was often to lament, not to spell, and it was a skill that he never mastered.

Wigglesworth had a particular burden for the districts of Bradford that were without a church and it was in one such area that he and Polly rented a small building and began holding services. Each Sunday, Polly would preach from the pulpit, while Wigglesworth looked after the children and 'carried the babies and the boots and everything', as well as waiting at the altar to lead those who came forward in the prayer of salvation. As he was to say, 'Polly's work was to put down the net and mine was to land the fish.'[1]

The first years of the Wigglesworths' married life were blissfully happy. They seemed to be a perfect match, for what one lacked the other had in abundance. Polly cared for the family, looked after the house, and did the accounts of the business, as well as being in great demand as a preacher and teacher, even for men's Bible classes. New members were being added to their little mission, and Wigglesworth's plumbing business was thriving, forged on his reputation for honesty and excellent workmanship. But then Wigglesworth had what was to be the only major lapse in his Christian life.

One year during the mid-1880s, severe winter weather gripped Bradford, and Wigglesworth and his two employees were inundated with calls to repair burst water pipes. Such was the havoc wreaked by the storms and freezing conditions during that winter that he was kept busy for the next two years repairing the damage. To keep up with the work, he started missing mid-week and Sunday services at the mission and devoted little time to prayer and Bible study, with the inevitable result that his relationship with God began to suffer. As his faith cooled, Polly, now burdened with pastoring the church alone, became more fervent. And as her zeal contrasted starkly with his spiritual indifference, it began to irritate him intensely. His innate weaknesses – his volcanic temper, impatience and tactlessness – previously held at bay by godly self-control, became more pronounced. Irritable and taciturn, he became critical and difficult to please. Polly's refusal to be provoked and retaliate only incensed him more until matters came to a head one night.

It was late and Polly had still not returned from a service at the mission. At Victor Road, Wigglesworth waited impatiently, brooding and mulling over what he was going to say to his all-too-independent wife. As she quietly tiptoed into the house, she was suddenly confronted by her husband, his face contorted with pent-up anger. 'I am the master of this 'ouse and I'm not 'aving you coming 'ome at so late an hour as this!' he roared. But in Mary Jane, Wigglesworth had met his match. Undaunted and with steely courage she quietly, but firmly replied, 'I know you're my husband, but Christ is my Master.' This apparent display of defiance enraged Wigglesworth, who grabbed hold of his wife and manhandled her out of the back door, slamming it shut, possibly accompanied by some choice oaths. In his haste, however, Wigglesworth, had forgotten that the front door was unlocked and thus Polly went around the side of the house and came in through the front laughing. Wigglesworth attempted to remain stern-faced, but her mirth was infectious and, despite himself, he found himself laughing at the absurdity of the situation.

Rather than nagging and cajoling her husband, Polly persisted in praying for him and in the months ahead she gently guided him towards rediscovering the love and devotion he had once had for God. It was a long and arduous journey that severely tested her faith, and their marriage, as Wigglesworth battled back from the brink of spiritual self-destruction, but resulted in his realisation that there were areas of his life that had not yet been yielded to God. The restoration of his faith would be accomplished in the coming months, but full sanctification would be a process that would take a number of years to complete, culminating in a spiritual epiphany in July 1893.

'I can remember the time,' said Wigglesworth reminiscing about that period of his life, 'when I used to go white with rage and shake all over with temper. I could hardly hold myself together. I waited on God for ten days. In those ten days, I was being emptied out and the life of the Lord Jesus Christ was being wrought into me. My wife testified of the transformation that took place in my life. "I never saw such a change," said my wife. "I have never been able to cook anything since that time that has not pleased him. Nothing is too hot or cold, everything is just right."' As he was to explain to his friend, George Stormont, 'God worked the old Wigglesworth nature out and began to work the new Jesus nature in.' Such was the transformation that one day his employees stayed behind after work and approached him, caps in hand, saying, 'We would like that spirit you have.'

His faith restored, Wigglesworth's new-found zeal knew no bounds. At work, he would witness to his customers, many of whom he led to Christ, as well as their employees. In his spare time, he would go from house to house, knocking on doors to share the gospel, and Saturday would find him out on the streets of Bradford conducting an evangelistic meeting in one of the main roads, with police protection – a practice he continued for twenty years. In winter he would often go out to the meeting without an overcoat, wearing his thinnest suit and flimsiest shoes so that he could experience the cold that the homeless and destitute endured.

The Saturday night open-air service would be followed by a prayer meeting. But the next morning, Wigglesworth would rise early to put things in order for Sunday's services. During the winter, he would attend to the heating of the mission building, clean the benches, praying over each one, and prepare the table for the communion service. He would conduct early morning prayers, before leading a pony through the streets of Bradford to attract a crowd of curious children who he would then invite to the morning service at the mission. The Sunday night service usually ended very late, and the fellowship would continue at Victor Road to well beyond midnight.

Wigglesworth's passion for souls became insatiable. Every day he sought to lead someone to Christ and was willing to wait hours for the opportunity. On one occasion, he stood at the roadside, asking God to lead him to the person He wanted him to witness to. The road was bustling with people and a myriad of horse-drawn vehicles, but Wigglesworth was determined to seek the right person and kept praying, 'Lord, I want the right man.' But no word came and Wigglesworth was becoming impatient. 'Lord, I don't have much time to waste,' he cried out silently. But still nothing.

An hour and a half slipped by and he was becoming increasingly agitated, when a horse and cart went by and God spoke to him that this was his man. Wigglesworth immediately chased after the cart, hoisted himself up beside the surprised driver and began his testimony. His presence was not appreciated. 'Why don't you go about your business? Why should you pick me out and talk to me?' said the driver tersely. The man's reaction threw Wigglesworth and made him wonder whether he had made a mistake. Stopping for a moment, he prayed quickly, 'Is this the right man, Lord?' God confirmed that it was and he continued to plead with the man to accept Christ as his Saviour.

As Wigglesworth persisted, an overwhelming conviction came upon the man and tears started to trickle down his cheeks. Convinced that the Holy Spirit was tugging at his soul, Wigglesworth sensed his work was done and, bidding him farewell, jumped off the cart. As he stood at the side of the road watching the cart disappear into the throng of traffic, he wondered to himself what would become of the man.

Three weeks later, Wigglesworth's mother said to him, 'Smith, have you been talking to someone about salvation?'

Wondering who she was referring to, Wigglesworth replied, 'I am always doing that, Mother.'

'Well, I visited a man last night. He was dying; he has been in bed for three weeks. I asked whether he would like someone to come and pray with him. He said, "The last time I was out, a young man got into my cart and spoke to me. I was very rough with him but he was very persistent. Anyhow, God convicted me of my sins and saved me."' His mother continued, 'That was the last time that man was out. He passed away in the night. He described the young man who talked with him and I could tell from his description that you were the one.'

The Wigglesworths' ministry in Bradford flourished and they were forced to move to larger premises on a number of occasions until, in 1889, they found a building in Bowland Street that became the Bowland Street Mission. As a beacon to the lost of Bradford, Wigglesworth purchased the tallest flagpole he could find, erected it outside the mission and hoisted a huge flag that could be seen for miles, one side of which was red, the other blue. In white letters were written on one side the scripture, 'I am the Lord that healeth thee,' on the other, 'Christ died for our sins.' The same verse was painted in giant letters on the wall behind the pulpit.

One day each week, Wigglesworth visited the city of Leeds, nine miles away, to purchase plumbing supplies and it was on one of his visits that he heard about divine healing meetings taking place at a mission called the Healing Home, which may have been connected to the Zion City movement.[2] This was later to become the Bridge Street Elim Church.

Wigglesworth began attending the Tuesday healing meetings on a regular basis, but was troubled that so many people were wearing glasses. True to form, he was unable to keep his thoughts to himself and in an accusatory tone declared, 'Why do you wear glasses if you believe in divine 'ealing?' This proved to be a bone of contention for Wigglesworth, but did not prevent him from coming, bringing members of his church with him. The leaders of the Healing Home chuckled as they saw him leading a procession of people with all kinds of ailments to the meeting. 'Here is Wigglesworth coming again and bringing a lot more,' they said to each other in amusement. 'If only he knew, he could get these people healed in Bradford just as easily as to get them healed in Leeds.'

At first, Wigglesworth said nothing to Polly about his visits to the meeting in Leeds, concerned that she would view it as fanaticism. But eventually she found out and, much to his relief, approved and even asked to attend a meeting herself where she received prayer and was healed. The Wigglesworths' association with the Healing Home brought them into contact with John Alexander Dowie,[3] founder of the Zion City movement, who held a series of heavily publicised meetings in London in 1900. According to the record, one of those baptised by triune immersion[4] by Dowie was 'Mrs M. J. Wigglesworth of Bradford'.

The leaders of the home recognised Wigglesworth's compassion for the sick and afflicted, and when they all decided to attend that year's Keswick Convention[5] they were unanimous in concluding that he was the only person capable of conducting the services while they were away. Wigglesworth protested that he had no experience of leading a healing service, but they persisted and assured him that all he had to do was take charge of the meeting, leaving him to assume that someone else would do the preaching. When he arrived for the first meetings of which he was in charge, the hall was full. Looking around he spotted a number of people he knew and enquired of each whether they were going to preach. To his horror, their replies were unanimous: 'No, you have been chosen and you must do it.' One can imagine that fear and panic gripped his mind as he contemplated having to do one of the things he dreaded most: speaking in public. Worse still, not expecting to preach, he had come unprepared. But, having agreed to lead the meetings, he felt that he had no choice but to step into the pulpit.

Such was his state of mind that in later years he could not recall what he preached that day, but the topic almost certainly included healing and, when he had concluded, fifteen people with various infirmities rose from their seats and came forward to the altar for prayer. First up was a big Scotsman who hobbled slowly towards the platform on crutches. As Wigglesworth observed the man inching towards him, his heart sank at the prospect of having to pray first for such an obvious case of infirmity. Falteringly and with little confidence, he prayed, laying his hands on the man and was stunned to see him drop his crutches and leap up and down ecstatically, completely healed. Emboldened, the others now stepped forward for prayer and all were healed. 'I am sure it was not my faith,' said Wigglesworth later, reflecting on this momentous moment, 'but it was God in His compassion coming to help me in that hour of need.'

Returning to Bradford, he held a healing meeting at the Bowland Street Mission. Twelve people came forward and all were healed, including one with a badly bitten tongue and a woman with an ulcer on her ankle and a large discharging sore. More meetings and more miracles followed, until Wigglesworth became renowned in Bradford and its environs for possessing a divine healing ministry.

One Sunday, a man who had a healing ministry of his own, preached at the mission and after the Sunday afternoon service was invited to the Wigglesworths' for tea.

While they sat in the front room munching sandwiches and discussing that morning's service, Polly said with a wry smile to the minister, 'What would you think of a man who preaches divine healing to others, yet he himself uses medical means every day in his life?' snatching a furtive glance at Wigglesworth who bowed his head, convicted. 'I should say that that man did not fully trust the Lord,' came the reply. Wigglesworth looked up and said meekly, 'When my wife was talking about one who preached divine healing to others and yet used other means himself, she was referring to me.' He then went on to explain that he had suffered from haemorrhoids since childhood and had used laxative salts ever since to induce a bowel movement. Wigglesworth knew only too well that his system was so dependent on the salts that if he stopped taking them that Sunday, by the following Wednesday he would suffer great pain and bleed profusely if he attempted a bowel movement.

Appealing to the minister to stand with him in prayer, Wigglesworth took a step of faith and discarded the salts. The day of reckoning came on Wednesday, and tense and nervous he strode solemnly to the bathroom where he anointed himself with oil, perched on the lavatory and said to God, 'Do what you want to, quickly.' In his own inimitable style, he was to describe what followed: 'God undertook. My bowels functioned that day like a baby's. God had perfectly healed me. From that day forward, my bowels have functioned perfectly without the use of any means whatsoever.'

Wigglesworth would often return from work, his hands black with grime and dash out of the house without even time to wash, so pressing were the petitions for prayer. One such request came from a Mr Clark, a Baptist minister, who came to Victor Road to plead for prayer for his dying wife. When Wigglesworth enquired searchingly why he couldn't believe that God would heal her, Clark replied shaking his head in despair, his voice brimming with pathos, 'Brother Wigglesworth, I cannot believe for her.' While Clark left, weeping, to return to his wife, Wigglesworth, a believer in the power of corporate prayer, sought the assistance of a man called Howe who had recently established a small mission in Bradford. It proved futile, for Howe, aghast at the prospect of praying for divine healing for someone who was near death, refused point-blank to accompany him to pray for Mrs Clark, begging Wigglesworth not to ask him again but adding, 'But I believe if you go, God will heal.'

Wigglesworth then turned to a man called Nichols who was notorious in Bradford for his vague, rambling prayers. Nichols was only too willing to accompany Wigglesworth, and together they set off to walk the one and a half miles to Clark's house. On the way, Wigglesworth advised him that once he commenced praying that he should continue until he had finished – a statement that he was to regret.

When they arrived, Mrs Clark was close to death and Wigglesworth immediately asked Nichols to pray. Seizing his chance with relish, Nichols began praying mournfully for the soon-to-be-bereaved husband and motherless children. Standing listening and becoming increasing agitated, Wigglesworth prayed silently and desperately, 'Stop him! Please Lord, stop this man praying!' But on and on Nichols droned until, unable to endure it any longer, Wigglesworth cried out, 'Stop him, Lord; I cannot stand this.' Startled, Nichols halted abruptly in mid-sentence, and glared at Wigglesworth. It was obvious to Wigglesworth that Nichols did not believe in divine healing, so he removed a half-pint bottle of olive oil from his hip pocket and put it behind his back in preparation for his turn to pray. After a friend had pointed out to him the scripture in

James 5:14 referring to anointing the sick with oil, he decided immediately that he had to obey the Word of God.

Inexplicably, Wigglesworth then appealed to Clark to pray, but Clark took his cue from Nichols and there followed another dreary monologue with Clark pleading for God's grace to sustain him in his bereavement. At the end of his tether, a wincing Wigglesworth could stand it no longer. 'Lord, stop him!' he bellowed so loudly that he could be heard outside the house. Clark flinched in fright, opened his eyes and stared at Wigglesworth, his mouth poised to utter the next word of his gloomy prayer.

Without further hesitation, Wigglesworth withdrew the cork from the bottle of oil, poured the glugging contents over the prostrate body of Mrs Clark and began praying earnestly for her healing. Clark and Nichols gaped at him and then each other in astonishment, as the viscose oil smothered Mrs Clark in a glistening shroud and splashed over the blankets leaving amber puddles. As he was to admit later, 'I was a novice at the time and I didn't know any better.' But as he continued to pray with feverish intensity, laying his hand on the brow of the dying woman, the miracle began to unfold:

> I was standing beside her at the top of the bed and looking towards the foot, when suddenly the Lord Jesus appeared. I had my eyes open gazing at Him. There he was at the foot of the bed. He gave me one of those gentle smiles . . . After a few moments he vanished, but something happened that day that changed my life. Mrs Clark was raised up and filled with life and lived to bring up a number of children; she outlived her husband many years.[6]

Not long following this miracle, Wigglesworth and Polly pledged that they would forsake medical treatment and trust in God alone for their health and healing. Gazing at each other, they declared solemnly, 'From henceforth, no medicine, no doctors, no drugs of any kind shall come into our house.'

Their resolve was soon to be put to the test when Wigglesworth began suffering from stabbing pains in his abdomen. This continued for six months, until one Sunday evening, while he was ministering at the Bowland Street Mission, he suddenly collapsed in agony. As the congregation gasped in shock, two men stepped forward quickly to help him to his feet and with an anxious Polly and bewildered children trailing behind, he staggered, ashen-faced and grimacing in pain, with the aid of the two members of his congregation, back to Victor Road.

Wigglesworth, Polly and the children prayed fervently through the night for his healing, but by ten o'clock the following morning his condition had worsened and he announced grimly to his wife, her face etched with fear and exhaustion, 'It seems to me that this is my home call. We have been praying all night and nothing has happened; I am worse. It does not seem as though anything can be done. You know our arrangement is that when we know we have received a home call, only then to save each other the embarrassment of having an inquest and the condemnation of outsiders, would we call a physician. To protect yourself, you should now call a physician. I leave it with you to do what you think should be done.'

Frantic with worry and surrounded by sobbing children, Polly broke down and wept, burying her face in her hands, before leaving the house, still weeping, in search of a doctor. When she returned, the doctor examined Wigglesworth and shook his head with an air of resignation. 'There is no hope whatsoever. He has had appendicitis for the last six months and the organs are in such shape that he is beyond hope.' Turning to Polly he said, 'I have a few calls to make, Mrs Wigglesworth. I will come and see you again later. The only hope is for him to have an immediate operation, but I am afraid your husband is too weak for that.' Polly showed the doctor to the door and returned to the bedroom.

Gazing at her bed-ridden husband, groaning in pain, Polly gripped the bed rail until her knuckles turned white and prayed desperately for guidance, tears trickling down her face, for it seemed that there was no hope. Suddenly, there was a knock at the door. Assuming that the doctor had returned early, she descended the stairs only to find that one of the children had already opened the door. Standing in the hallway were an elderly woman and a young man clutching his cloth cap in one hand and a Bible in the other. The woman explained to Polly that they had heard that Wigglesworth was gravely ill and had felt compelled by the Lord to come and pray for his healing. Polly led them to the bedroom and left the room to attend to the children

While the old woman began praying fervently, the young man knelt on the bed and, placing his hands on Wigglesworth, cried, 'Come out you devil, in the name of Jesus!' Recalled Wigglesworth, 'There was no chance for an argument or for me to tell him that I would never believe that there was a devil inside me. The thing had to go in the name of Jesus and it went. I was healed instantly.' (James Salter commented that the young man drove his fist into Wigglesworth's stomach and it may be from this time that Wigglesworth began the practice of applying physical force when he prayed for the sick.)

Thanking the two prayer warriors before they left the room to enable him to get dressed. Wigglesworth got up and went downstairs to a shocked Polly who could only cry, 'Oh, you are up!'

'It's all right, Wife, I'm 'ealed,' replied Wigglesworth impassively, reassuring her and hugging the children. He then enquired, 'Any work in?'

Polly, still in a daze, informed him that there was a woman in urgent need of some plumbing, giving him the address. With that, Wigglesworth picked up his bag of tools and left the house, leaving Polly and the children to rejoice over his miraculous healing.

Not long after, the doctor returned, put his silk hat on the hall table and was just mounting the stairs when Polly called out to him that her husband had gone out to work. Shocked, he replied, 'You will never see him alive again. They will bring him back a corpse.'

Recounting the story on many occasions later, Wigglesworth was to say with a twinkle in his eye, 'Well the "corpse" has been going up and down the world preaching the gospel these many years since that time. I have laid hands on people with appendicitis in almost every part of the world and never knew of a case not instantly healed.'

Once, when Wigglesworth came back late from work he found an urgent call had come for him to pray for a girl dying of tuberculosis. When he arrived he looked at the girl, her breath coming in short, strangled gasps and realised that her only hope was a miracle. Turning to her mother, he told her that she and her other children should go to bed and leave him to pray alone for her daughter. Ever since he had prayed for Mrs Clark he had realised the difficulties of praying in an atmosphere saturated with human sympathy and unbelief. When they refused to leave the room, Wigglesworth put on his overcoat and said brusquely, 'Goodbye, I'm off.' As he was about to open the front door they begged him to stay and agreed to comply with his demand.

They all went to bed and I stayed and that was surely a time as I knelt by that bed face to face with the devil. But God can change the hardest situation and make you know that He is almighty.

Then the fight came. It seemed as if the heavens were brass. I prayed from 11 to 3.30 in the morning. I saw the glimmering light on the face of the sufferer and saw her pass away. The devil said, 'Now you are done for. You have come from Bradford and the girl has died on your hands.' I said, 'It can't be. God did not send me here for nothing'. This is a time to change strength. I remembered that passage which said, 'Men ought always to pray and not faint.' Death had taken place but I knew that my God was all-powerful and He that had split the Red Sea is just the same today. It was a time when I would not have 'No', and God said 'Yes'.

I looked at the window and at that moment, the face of Jesus appeared. It seemed as if a million rays of light were coming from His face. He looked at the young woman who had just passed away. As He did so, the colour came back into her face. She rolled over and fell asleep. Then I had a glorious time.

In the morning, the young lady woke early, put on her robe and walked to the piano. She started to play and sing a wonderful song. Her mother and family and the sister and brother had all come down to listen. The Lord had undertaken. A miracle had been wrought.

On 13 February 1904, a man so vile that even the most depraved members of Bradford's underworld would shun his company, walked into the Bowland Street Mission. James Berry (1862–1913) had been the Crown's Public Executioner from 1884 to 1892 and had been responsible for the execution of 134 men and women. He told Wigglesworth later that he believed that the demon spirits that inhabited the murderers he hanged entered him at their death and that, consequently, he had become possessed by a legion of demons.

Despite retiring from his post of executioner twelve years before, Berry was still haunted night and day by images of those he executed. Suffering from bouts of acute depression and drinking heavily, he decided one day that he would end his torment by throwing himself into the path of an oncoming train. But as he sat dejectedly on the platform of Bradford's Midland Station preparing to end his life, Berry was approached by a young man who had been converted at the Bowland Street Mission the day before. The man had determined that each day he would lead at least one person to Christ and as Berry poured out his heart, weeping, the man invited him to come to the mission that afternoon.

Berry duly arrived at the mission, and for two and a half hours, recalled Wigglesworth, 'he was literally sweating under conviction and you could see the vapour rising from him'. As Wigglesworth and members of the congregation prayed, the demons were exorcised. Finally, deliverance came and Berry surrendered his life to Christ.

Wigglesworth then prayed fervently, 'Lord, tell me what to do.' The answer came: 'Don't leave him. Go home with him.' He obeyed and returned with Berry to his house. 'I tell you there was a difference in that home,' recalled Wigglesworth. 'Even the cat knew the difference. . . . There were two sons in that house and one of them said to his mother, "Mother, what is up in our house? It was never like this before. It is so peaceful. What is it?" She told him, "Father has got saved." The other son was struck by the same thing.' Following his conversion, James Berry became an outstanding itinerant evangelist, leading hundreds to Christ, and a prominent campaigner for the abolition of the death penalty.

Over the years, preaching in the streets of Bradford on a Saturday had helped Wigglesworth overcome, to some degree, his inability to speak in public, but he still stammered and stumbled as soon as he stepped into the pulpit at the Bowland Street Mission. Not one to give up easily, Polly was determined to train her husband in the art of public speaking and continually made announcements that the following Sunday he would preach, convinced that with practise he could overcome his limitations.

Said Wigglesworth: 'My wife tried her best to make me someone. She could not do it. Her heart, her love, her desire were right, for she did her best to make me a preacher. She used to say, "Now, Father, you could do it if you would. I want you to preach next Sunday."

'I tried everything to get ready. I don't know what I did not try. It would be best not to tell you what I tried. I had as many notes as would suit a parson for a week! But when I got up to preach, I gave out my text and then said, "If anybody can preach, now is your chance, for I am done."' Finally, after yet another attempt at preaching ended in failure, Wigglesworth announced to Polly one Sunday gruffly, 'I'll never do that again!'

Little could Smith Wigglesworth have imagined then that the time would come when he would preach without stumbling or stuttering to thousands from platforms and pulpits around the world. The year was 1907 and an event was about to take place that would transform Wigglesworth and his ministry forever.

Chapter Four

BAPTISED BY FIRE

As the twentieth century dawned, Smith Wigglesworth had every reason to feel a sense of fulfilment. The Bowland Street Mission was growing and nurturing some fine young ministers; an evangelistic and healing ministry that extended beyond the confines of Bradford had been established; and he felt that his cup was overflowing spiritually. As he said himself, 'We thought that we had got all that was coming to us on spiritual lines.'

Up until then, the Wigglesworths accepted the Holiness doctrine espoused by Bible teachers at the annual Keswick Convention of a second work of grace that was often described as the baptism of the Holy Spirit, but which differed from the Pentecostal view of the experience. 'My wife and I always believed in scriptural holiness,' said Wigglesworth, 'but I was conscious of much carnality in myself. A really holy man [probably Richard Reader Harris, leader of the Pentecostal League of Prayer] once came to preach for us and he spoke of what it means to be entirely sanctified. He called it a very definite work of grace subsequent to the new birth. As I waited on the Lord for ten days in prayer, handing my body over to him as a living sacrifice according to Romans 12:1–2, God surely did something for me . . . We counted that as the baptism in the Spirit. And so, at our Bowland Street Mission, we stood for healing and holiness.'

That event took place in July 1893, but Wigglesworth was aware that, despite the miraculous healings that occurred when he prayed for the sick, the signs about which he read as he pored over the Book of Acts and Mark 16 in the Bible, were not fully present in his own ministry. Thus, when he heard that speaking in tongues and the gifts of the Spirit were reportedly being manifested at All Saints Church, an Anglican church in the district of Monkwearmouth in Sunderland, he was both deeply moved and excited.

The church was pastored by Revd Alexander Boddy (1854–1930) who was well acquainted with the Pentecostal Revival, having travelled to Wales in 1904 to observe the Welsh Revival and to the Azusa Street Mission in Los Angeles, the birthplace of the Pentecostal revival in America. However, it was the ministry of Thomas Bell Barratt, a Methodist minister of British descent from Norway, that had made the most impact on him. Boddy visited Barratt's mission in Oslo, and wrote when he returned, 'My four days in Christiana [Oslo] can never be forgotten. I stood with Evan Roberts in Tonypandy,[1] but have never witnessed such scenes as those in Norway.'

Boddy discovered that Barratt was on his way to the United States and invited him to stop over en route to hold meetings at his church in Sunderland. Barratt arrived at the end of August and stayed for seven weeks, during which time a number of people at All Saints were baptised by the Spirit and spoke in tongues. After about a month, the newspapers became aware of the story and the church was suddenly besieged by reporters and those eager to receive the baptism themselves.

To find out more about what was occurring in Sunderland, Wigglesworth wrote to two former members of the Bowland Street Mission who had moved to the city. Their response was not very encouraging. They warned him that the manifestations were of the devil, and when he arrived in Sunderland, they came to see him, accompanied by a woman of high spiritual repute, to try to dissuade him from visiting the church. But after hearing their arguments and a period of prayer, Wigglesworth resolved that the only way to discover the truth was to go and see for himself.

He arrived at All Saints Church for the Saturday night meeting with great anticipation. But it proved to be a huge disappointment for Wigglesworth, who the night before at the mission had observed members of his own congregation falling prostrate under the power of the Holy Spirit. Never slow to express his feelings in public, he declared bluntly, 'I've come from Bradford and I want this experience of speaking in tongues like they 'ad on the day of Pentecost. But I do not understand why our meetings are on fire but yours don't seem to be so.' Embarrassed by his outburst, members of the congregation asked him politely to sit down and refrain from causing a disturbance. But such was his insatiable hunger for the things of God that he found it impossible to suppress his feelings for long.

During one of the meetings that followed, a man stood up and testified that he had spoken in tongues after three weeks of waiting on God. Wigglesworth listened intently, until he could contain his excitement no longer. 'Let's 'ear those tongues,' he interrupted loudly, his eyes bright with expectation, 'That's what I came for. Let's 'ear it!' Heads turned to glare disapprovingly at Wigglesworth and one man replied exasperated, 'When you are baptised in the Spirit you will speak in tongues.' For Wigglesworth, who was absolutely convinced that he had been baptised in the Spirit, this was a challenge that could not go unanswered.

'I am baptised and there's no one 'ere that can persuade me that I'm not,' he replied defiantly, daring anyone to contradict him. But when he described what happened during his ten days secluded with God they assured him, perhaps warily, fearing his vehement denials, that this was not the baptism as on the day of Pentecost.

On Sunday morning, Wigglesworth rose early to attend a prayer meeting at the local Salvation Army hall. Three times during that meeting, Wigglesworth fell to the floor prostrate under the power of the Spirit. Conscious of the stares of those around him and embarrassed that he might be misunderstood, he got onto his knees to pray. Following the service, a Salvation Army captain enquired where he was from. When Wigglesworth told him that he was from Bradford and that he had come to Sunderland to witness people speaking in tongues, he was warned, as he had been before, that it was a satanic manifestation. He was invited to preach that afternoon, and after the service they urged him to avoid the Pentecostal 'people' and not to return to All Saints Church.

But Wigglesworth refused to be swayed and, ignoring their advice, attended the meeting at the vestry that night and then again on Monday morning. By his own admission he disrupted the meeting and, by now, his constant interruptions were beginning to get on people's nerves. After the service, a missionary from India, incensed by Wigglesworth's lack of sensitivity, followed him out of the vestry and confronted him. 'You are spoiling all the meetings,' he fumed. 'You claim to be baptised with the Holy Spirit and yet you are creating a disturbance at every meeting that you attend.' Wigglesworth defended himself vigorously and a heated argument ensued. They were both staying at the same hotel, but when they returned after the meeting, they walked back on opposite sides of the road.[2]

On the Tuesday night, Wigglesworth attended an all-night tarrying service conducted by the Revd Boddy, but by 2.30 a.m. the next morning, Boddy decided to close the meeting. As an ironic twist, Wigglesworth discovered that he had left his hotel room key in the suit he had changed out of before the meeting. The missionary from India, with whom he had had a confrontation, offered, perhaps with a few misgivings, to let him stay with him for the night. It was evidently a time of forgiveness and reconciliation for, according to Wigglesworth, they spent the early hours of the morning praying and were greatly blessed.

Wigglesworth had now been in Sunderland for four days and yet he had neither experienced speaking in tongues nor spoken in them himself. With urgent requests coming in for his plumbing services, he reluctantly decided to return to Bradford. Deflated, he stopped by at the vicarage to bid farewell to the Revd Boddy and found Mary Boddy in the library. Betraying his disappointment, he explained to her that although he was returning to Bradford he was yet to speak in tongues.

'I cannot rest any longer, I must 'ave these tongues,' cried Wigglesworth in exasperation.

'Brother Wigglesworth, it's not the tongues you need but the baptism,' replied Mrs Boddy calmly. 'If you will allow God to baptise you, the other will be all right.'

As ever, Wigglesworth was adamant that he had already received the baptism, yet he was desperate enough to ask her to pray and lay her hands on him.

She complied with his request, but then a persistent knocking at the door compelled her to leave the room. As she closed the door, the fire of the Holy Spirit suddenly fell on Wigglesworth and, overcome with joy, he cried out, 'Clean! Clean! Clean!' as he became conscious of being cleansed and purified. Describing the event later,

Wigglesworth said, 'I was given a vision in which I saw the Lord Jesus Christ. I beheld the empty cross and I saw Him exalted at the right hand of God the Father. I could no longer speak in English but I began to praise Him in other tongues as the Spirit of God gave utterance. I knew then, although I might have received anointings previously, that now, at last, I had received the real baptism in the Holy Spirit as they received on the day of Pentecost.'

Filled to overflowing with the Holy Spirit and bursting to tell someone what had happened, Wigglesworth darted out of the library, found Mary Boddy, promptly kissed her and then related to her his remarkable experience. He then went straight to a meeting that was in progress in the vestry of All Saints Church. The Revd Boddy was speaking when Wigglesworth quietly entered and sat down, but, fidgeting with excitement and unable to restrain himself, he interrupted Boddy and pleaded to be allowed to speak about his experience.

Permission was granted by Boddy who, peering closely at Wigglesworth, was struck by the radiance of his countenance. As the words describing his baptism tumbled excitedly and incoherently out of Wigglesworth's mouth, the others listened intently. At the end of Wigglesworth's account, a wave of discontented murmuring swept the vestry, before someone stood up and said, 'We have been rebuking this man because he was so intensely hungry, but he has come in for a few days and has received the baptism and some of us have been waiting here for months and have not yet received.' According to Wigglesworth, it was not long before fifty people in the congregation had received the baptism of the Spirit, including the Revd Alexander Boddy himself.

Ironically, a few months later, Stanley Frodsham would receive the baptism of the Spirit kneeling on the same spot as Wigglesworth, in the same room and prayed for by the same person – Mary Boddy. All three would soon organise Pentecostal conventions: Wigglesworth at the Bowland Street Mission which would continue until 1919; Boddy in Sunderland between 1908 and 1914; and Frodsham in Bournemouth, on the south coast of England, in 1909.

Before he left Sunderland, Wigglesworth sent a telegram to Victor Road, Bradford (a post office was opposite his house): 'I have received the baptism of the Holy Spirit and have spoken in tongues.' While on the train, Wigglesworth was suddenly plagued with doubt about his experience. 'Are you going to take this to Bradford?' mocked a satanic voice. The battle raged in his mind until, unable to endure it any longer, he suddenly shouted out loud, 'Yes, I'm taking it!' startling his fellow passengers. Wigglesworth was oblivious to their stares as joy flooded his being, but he sensed the contest was just beginning.

When he arrived home, his youngest son ran to meet him and asked excitedly, eyes bright with anticipation, 'Father, have you been speaking in tongues?'

'Yes, George,' replied Wigglesworth.

'Then let's hear you!'

But, as Wigglesworth was to explain later, he could not because he believed that he was yet to receive the gift of tongues. He was fiercely opposed to requests to demonstrate tongues and would condemn such practices as 'activities of the flesh'.

By this time, Polly had appeared with a steely glint in her eye: 'So you've been speaking in tongues have you?' she said scornfully, looking him up and down with arms folded. All Wigglesworth could manage in reply was a meek, 'Yes.'

'I want you to understand,' continued Polly, 'that I am as much baptised as you are and I don't speak in tongues.

I have been preaching for twenty years and you have sat beside me on the platform, but on Sunday you will preach yourself and I'll see what there is in it.' With that, she disappeared into the kitchen, leaving a shaken Wigglesworth to ponder the battle that lay ahead.

The next morning after his baptism he went to work as usual and as he walked down a crowded street he suddenly started speaking in tongues. People looked round surprised and some gardeners trimming a hedge peered over the top to see from where the strange gabble was coming, to find, to their astonishment, that it was Wigglesworth the plumber. Wigglesworth was determined that he was not going to walk any farther until God gave him the interpretation and then out it came: 'Over the hills and far away before the brink of day the Lord thy God will send thee forth and prosper all thy way.'

There was no backing down from the challenge laid down by his wife and on the following Sunday, Polly, to the surprise of the congregation, sat, not on the platform with her husband as she always did, but on one of the long benches at the back of the hall. All eyes were on Wigglesworth as he slowly walked the length of the mission hall to preach that morning. By now, the whole congregation had heard that their leader had been baptised by the Spirit and had spoken in other tongues and all were eager not only for him to demonstrate the phenomenon, but to observe what difference it had made. As he mounted the three steps leading up to the platform he was still wondering nervously what he was going to preach, when suddenly the gentle voice of the Holy Spirit whispered to him that he should begin with the words in the book of Isaiah 61: 'The Spirit of the Lord is upon me; because the LORD hath anointed me to preach good tidings unto the meek; he hath sent me to bind up the brokenhearted, to proclaim liberty to the captives, and the opening of the prison to them that are bound.'

Instead of his usual, faltering, stumbling efforts, Wigglesworth preached with fluency and power, the words gushing forth from his mouth like a torrent, to the astonishment of the congregation. 'Suddenly I felt that I had prophetic utterances which were flowing like a river by the power of the Holy Spirit,' said Wigglesworth, describing the experience later.

At the rear of the hall, Polly was becoming increasingly agitated, moving from one part of the bench to another. Then she said in a voice loud enough for everyone in the congregation to hear, 'That's not my Smith, Lord, that's not my Smith!' continuing with 'Amazing, amazing,' and 'What's happened to the man?'

As Wigglesworth was announcing the last hymn, the secretary of the mission rose from his seat and declared, 'I want what our leader has received.' He then went to sit down, but missed his seat and went crashing to the floor. Then Wigglesworth's eldest son Seth stood and said he also wanted what his father had received and, remarkably, the same thing occurred. It was not long before there were eleven people on the floor of the mission all helpless with laughter. This proved to be the beginning of a great outpouring of the Holy Spirit in Bradford in which hundreds received the baptism and spoke in other tongues. Suddenly, Wigglesworth was deluged with invitations to preach, including one from a Lancashire factory owner, who closed his factory from one o'clock to eleven o'clock at night to enable Wigglesworth to preach to his workers.

But Wigglesworth perceived that God had a greater purpose still for his baptism, other than an ability to preach. He prayed earnestly for revelation, and then the answer came dramatically. One day he arrived home from work and was met by an anxious Polly.

'Which way did you come in?' she enquired agitatedly.

'By the back door,' he replied, curious as to why she should ask such a question.

'There is a woman upstairs and she has brought an eighty-year-old man to be prayed for. He is raving up there and a great crowd has gathered outside the front door, ringing the doorbell and wanting to know what is going on in the house'

As if on cue, the doorbell trilled again, followed by banging and muffled cries.

By now Wigglesworth had become aware of the pitiful wailing that was emanating from the floor above. As he listened, he heard that familiar voice speak silently to his inner man, 'This is what I baptised you for.' Removing his coat, he scaled the stairs two at a time, with Polly following, and carefully opened the door. There, kneeling on the floor, was the man, his head in his wrinkled hands.

'I am lost! I am lost! I have committed the unpardonable sin. I am lost! I am lost!' he sobbed, his shoulders heaving as his wife, weeping also, tried to console him.

'Smith, what should we do?' cried Polly, alarmed.

Wigglesworth turned and gazed at her, his eyes blazing with intensity, and then, back to the man. 'Come out you lying spirit,' he thundered.

Immediately, the man was delivered and, smiling through his tears, he began praising God loudly.

Polly, having witnessed the astonishing transformation in her husband, was among those who received the baptism soon after he preached at Bowland Street, and together she and Wigglesworth ministered all over the country as pioneers of the Pentecostal message. One of the places at which they first preached was a primitive Methodist chapel in a village in Shropshire. As Polly spoke from the pulpit, the fire of God fell on the congregation and many were baptised by the Spirit. However, as was often the case in the years to come, there were some who fiercely opposed the Pentecostal experience and were highly critical.

The anointing that now rested on Wigglesworth was causing some startling reactions among those with whom he was coming into contact. 'Wherever I went,' recalled Wigglesworth, 'conviction seemed to be upon people.' The morning following a meeting at the chapel, Wigglesworth decided to explore the village and walked into the grocery shop. Immediately the three people in the shop were convicted of their sins and accepted Christ as their Saviour. Leaving the three behind, he continued walking up the road and saw two women in a field carrying buckets. He called out to them, 'Are you saved?' A powerful conviction immediately seized the women and they dropped their buckets, fell on their knees and began praying fervently with Wigglesworth for Christ's forgiveness.

There was a stone quarry near the village, and Wigglesworth decided to preach to the men who worked there. As they hewed out stones from the rock, he spoke passionately, Bible in hand, of Christ and the Cross, and a number of the men knelt in their soiled work clothes with him to pray the prayer of salvation.

As he was on his way back to the village, he passed a public house. 'Just as I was nearing it [the saloon] two men drove by in a two-wheel vehicle, and I never have seen men with such evil faces. They looked the very picture of the devil. I did not know who they were but as they came near they cursed me and tried to slash their whip at me. It seemed like a whiff from the pit. They shouted so loudly that the landlord and landlady at the hotel and five people came out of that saloon and dashed at me like mad dogs, cursing and swearing, though I had not spoken a word to them. But I did not fear their assault. I cried out instantly, "In the name of Jesus, in the power of the blood of Jesus, I drive you back into your den." They rushed back into the hotel and I went in and preached Jesus to them.'

Returning to Bradford, Wigglesworth received a succession of telegrams pleading for him to go to a village nine miles from Grantham, a town in Lincolnshire, to pray for a young man called Matthew who was dying. Matthew had come to the mission in Bradford before and had been healed of a serious foot condition. When Wigglesworth arrived, he was met at the door of the farmhouse by the man's weeping mother, who informed him that he was too late. Unmoved, Wigglesworth replied, 'God has never sent me anywhere too late.'

He found the man in bed with his face to a wall; his breath coming in short gasps. Speaking to Wigglesworth in a barely audible whisper, he told him that he thought he would die if he dared turn over, so weak was his heart.

'Well, in that case, I'll pray for the Lord to strengthen you,' replied Wigglesworth.

'I knew that this case was beyond all human hopes,' recalled Wigglesworth, 'and so I lay awake most of the night praying. I got up very early the next morning and went out to an adjoining field to pray, for I was very much burdened about this case. There in that field God gave me a revelation that this had to be something new in my life.'

It was a Sunday morning and Wigglesworth attended the morning service at the Methodist church in the village. When he informed the congregation who he was and why he had come, they invited him to conduct the service. As he revealed the vision that God had given him for the young man's healing, the congregation's faith rose and they cried out in unison, 'Matthew will be raised up!'

Wigglesworth, commenting on the incident later said, 'That led me to see that faith could be created in others just as it had been created in me . . . '

Wigglesworth returned to the house emboldened and told Matthew, 'When I place my hands on you, the glory of the Lord will fill the place till I shall not be able to stand. I shall be helpless on the floor.' He then asked Matthew's parents to put his socks on and then, as was always the case in such circumstances, requested that they leave the room and close the door behind them so that he could be 'shut in with God'. Gazing at Matthew's motionless, wheezing form, he placed his hands on him:

I prayed for the vision to be made good and instantly, the moment I touched the young man, the power of God filled the room and was so powerful that I fell to the floor. My nose and my mouth were touching the floor and I lay there in the glory for a quarter of an hour. All that while, Matthew in the bed was shouting, 'Lord, this is for Thy glory! This is for Thy glory!' The bed simply shook, as did everything in the room, by the power of God. Matthew's strength, his life and his heart (which was considered the weakest thing about him) were all renewed. I was still on the floor in the glory when he arose from his bed and began to dress. After he was dressed, he began to walk up and down the room shouting, 'I'm raised up for Thy glory! I'm raised up for Thy glory!' Opening the door, he shouted, 'Dad, God has healed me. I'm healed!' The glory filled the kitchen; the father and mother fell down, and the daughter who had been brought from the asylum and whose mind was still affected, was made perfectly whole that day.[3]

Matthew's healing sparked a revival in the village, and when Wigglesworth was about to return to Bradford, many pleaded with him to stay, saying, 'Please come back, please come back and stop with us longer next time.'

It was during this period that another remarkable healing occurred. Wigglesworth was in Wales when he heard the story of a man who had climbed a mountain to pray and returned to his village with a face that shone like an angel's. Wigglesworth decided to emulate the man and climb to the top of the same mountain to pray. 'As I went up in to this mountain and spent the day in the presence of the Lord,' said Wigglesworth, describing the experience, 'His wonderful power seemed to envelop and saturate me.'

Two years before, two young men from a village near Llanelli in South Wales, visited the Bowland Street Mission and remarked to Wigglesworth, 'We would not be surprised if the Lord brings you down to Wales to raise our Lazarus.' They explained to him that the leader of their church had worked as a tin miner and lay pastor, preaching and ministering at night and on Sundays, until exhausted he had collapsed, having contracted tuberculosis. For four years he had been a helpless cripple, bedridden and having to be spoon-fed.

Sitting on the summit of the mountain praying, Wigglesworth heard the silent voice of God speaking to his inner man, 'I want you to go and raise Lazarus.' He descended the mountain and sent a message to the village that he was coming to pray for Lazarus. But when he arrived, the man to whom he had addressed the card informed him gloomily, 'The moment you see him, you will be ready to go home. Nothing will keep you here.'

When Wigglesworth at last saw Lazarus, he realised that what he was told was not an exaggeration. 'The man [Lazarus] was helpless. He was nothing but a mass of bones with skin stretched over them. There was no life to be seen. Everything in him spoke of decay.' Wigglesworth tried to instil some faith into him, but someone had prayed for his healing two years before and had failed to raise him up and now he refused to believe. 'There was not an atom of faith there,' recalled Wigglesworth. Neither could he find much faith in the village. When he asked who would be willing to join him in prayer for the man, none responded. Eventually, he was able to persuade the couple who had given he and his companion lodging to join them the next day. Refusing to eat dinner, Wigglesworth fasted and prayed and then went to bed. That night the battle commenced:

> When I got to bed it seemed as if the devil tried to place on me everything that he had placed on that poor man. When I awoke, I had a cough and all the weakness of a tubercular patient. I rolled out of bed and . . . cried out to God to deliver me from the power of the devil. I shouted loud enough to wake everybody in the house, but nobody was disturbed. God gave victory and I got back in bed as free as ever. At five o'clock the Lord awakened me and said, 'Don't break bread until you break it round my table.' At six o'clock he gave me these words, 'And I will raise him up.' I put my elbow into the fellow who was sleeping with me and said, 'Do you hear? The Lord says that he will raise him up.'

The next morning at eight o'clock, Wigglesworth, his companion, the couple they were staying with, and four others who had had a change of heart and decided to accompany them, arrived at Lazarus' house. They stood around the bed and formed a chain by linking hands, including Lazarus himself. 'We are just going to use the name of Jesus,' Wigglesworth told them.

> We knelt down and whispered that one word, 'Jesus! Jesus! Jesus!' The power of God fell and then it lifted. Five times the

power of God fell and then it lifted. Five times the power of God fell and then it remained. But the man in the bed was unmoved. Two years previously, someone had come along and had tried to raise him up and the devil had used his lack of success as a means of discouraging Lazarus.

I said, 'I don't care what the devil says. If God says he will raise him up, it must be so. Forget everything else except what God says about Jesus.'

The sixth time the power fell and the sick man's lips began moving and the tears began to fall. I said, 'The power of God is here. It is yours to accept.' Then he made a confession: 'I have been bitter in my heart and I know I have grieved the Spirit of God.'

As we again said 'Jesus! Jesus! Jesus!' the bed shook and the man shook. I told the people who were with me that they could go downstairs. 'This is all God. I'm not going to help him.' I sat and watched that man get up and dress himself, and then we sang the doxology as he walked down the steps.

The epilogue to the story was that news of Lazarus' healing spread beyond the confines of the village to the whole district, and as he testified to what happened, many were converted.

It was at some point after his Pentecostal baptism that Wigglesworth decided to give up working as a plumber and devote all his time to ministry. It appears, however, that the business that he had built up continued, as it was noted in 1942 that his eldest son, Seth, as well as being the treasurer of Bradford Elim Church, was also a director of the family plumbing business.

Requests were coming in from all over the country for Wigglesworth's ministry, and he found that he was called away from Bradford so often that each time he returned, he had less business. The final straw came when he attended a convention in the town of Preston in Lancashire. There was a severe frost, and before he left he visited his regular customers and ensured that their water pipes were covered to prevent them from bursting. While he was at the convention, the frost started to thaw and the pipes began to expand and burst as the temperature rose. Telegrams arrived from people pleading with Wigglesworth to return to Bradford to repair the pipes, but by the time he got back, all his customers had been forced to seek help from other plumbers. The exception was a widow whose house was flooded and who was unable to get assistance. Wigglesworth repaired her pipes and one of her ceilings, which had caved in. When she enquired how much she owed him, he replied, 'I won't receive any pay from you. I'll make this an offering to the Lord as my last plumbing job.'

Wigglesworth was willing to give up his successful business, but he had one condition: 'I promised Him at that time that I would obey Him implicitly, but I laid down the condition that my shoe heels must never be a disgrace, and I must never have to wear trousers with the knees out. I said to the Lord, "If either of these things take place, I'll go back to plumbing".' But he never needed to, for as he was to confirm, 'He has never failed to supply all my needs.'

One day, Wigglesworth was reading Luke 14:13–14 in his beloved New Testament: 'When thou makest a feast, call the poor, the maimed, the lame, the blind: And thou shalt be blessed; for they cannot recompense thee: for thou shalt be recompensed at the resurrection of the just.' As he read and reread the verses out loud, he suddenly had a revelation. He darted out of the room to show Polly and, bubbling with excitement, announced that they were going to do just as the Bible said – they were going to hold a banquet for the poor, but with a difference.

A plan was quickly devised to ensure the event was well organised, to avoid any confusion. This included employing two people to tour the slums and back streets of Bradford giving out invitations and announcing through loudhailers the forthcoming banquet and entertainment at the Bowland Street Mission.

When the day of the event came, Wigglesworth went to fetch a woman who was unable to walk. First, Wigglesworth had to repair the broken wheel of her bath chair. He helped her into the chair and they set off, but the wheel gave way again. As he performed a makeshift repair, he told her, 'Well you'll never want it again, anyhow.' They turned into Bowland Street and as they neared the mission, Wigglesworth stopped dead in his tracks. Before him was an incredible sight: an army of people, some caked in filth from head to toe, were either milling outside the mission or advancing like a human tide towards it. The blind were being led by the hand, invalids and the infirm were being pushed in wheelchairs, while others hobbled on crutches. Some were swathed in bandages, a few, ashen-faced and near death, were being carried on stretchers and still others had tumours and massive dome-shaped goitres. A ragged mass of diseased humanity thronged into the mission, as members of the congregation struggled to keep order.

As Wigglesworth stood in the street and gazed at the astonishing scene, he began to weep with body convulsing sobs, not only at surveying the overwhelming needs of the people, but also at the expectation of what God was going to do that day, a day that he was later to describe as the greatest of his life up to that point.

Inside the hall, the people were seated around long trestle tables covered in crisp, white table cloths – already soiled by a patchwork of stains – loaded with steaming tureens of soup, joints of roasted pork, beef and mutton, fluffy Yorkshire puddings and plates piled high with fresh, crusty bread. Soon the mission hall was a hive of noise and activity: the high-pitched whine of excited chatter; babies bawling and children squabbling over the choicest morsels; the clatter of cutlery and crockery and the glint of carving knives, as emaciated men and women hacked ravenously at the meat, stuffing their mouths with food in their haste to fill their empty stomachs.

When everyone had had their fill, Wigglesworth mounted the platform and announced that the main event of the evening was about to commence. It took him several attempts to attract their attention, but eventually the babble of noise ebbed to hushed whispers. The first person up was a man who had spent years in a wheelchair but could now walk. Then came a woman who had haemorrhaged blood but had been healed the day before she was to be operated on. Next up was a man who had been partially paralysed by a stroke. The doctors had given up on him, but Jesus had healed him. And so it continued for an hour and a half, as person after person gave their testimony, while many in the audience wept openly. Finally, Wigglesworth himself addressed the audience: 'We have been entertaining you today. But we are going to have another meeting next Saturday and you people who today are bound, some of you in wheelchairs, are going to entertain us by the stories of freedom that you have received today by the name of Jesus Christ.' Then Smith Wigglesworth made, possibly for the first time, the declaration that would be pronounced from platforms around the world: "Oo wants to be 'ealed?' Barely had his booming voice ceased reverberating around the rafters of the hall than there was a sudden surge towards the platform of people desperate to receive his prayers. Removing his jacket, Wigglesworth stepped off the platform and plunged in among them.

There was pandemonium as people shrieked and wept as they were healed. A young man who had been having epileptic fits for eighteen years was instantly delivered as

Wigglesworth laid his hands on him. He came to another young man who was bent double, and discerning a spirit of infirmity, cast the spirit out and immediately the man straightened up and started weeping with joy.

At the back of the hall was a man holding his limp son whose frail form was encased in thin iron. Desperate to get the boy to the platform, but failing to find a way through the seething mass of people, he hoisted the boy above his head and passed him onto outstretched hands. The boy was handed to one person after another over the heads of the crowd until he reached the platform and was placed at Wigglesworth's feet. Wigglesworth tenderly anointed the boy with oil, laid his hands on him and declared that he was to be healed in the name of Jesus. Immediately, the power of God touched him and he cried out, 'Papa, Papa, Papa. It's going all over me! It's going all over me! It's going all over me!' Eyes bright with anticipation, Wigglesworth ordered the father to remove the iron case. With feverish hands, the man unclipped the case to reveal that his son had been completely healed. As the boy gazed at his limbs, his face glowing with wonder, his father, beside himself with joy, weeping and laughing, hugged the little boy tightly.

The woman whom Wigglesworth had wheeled into the hall in a broken bath chair was also miraculously healed that night. She, Wigglesworth, Polly and others from the mission walked home, chattering excitedly about the incredible events that had taken place that day. When they arrived at the woman's house, they followed her in and watched jubilantly as she scaled the stairs to her bedroom, praising God as she went. With a final farewell, they left the woman's house and as they strolled up the street back to Victor Road, they could still hear faint cries of 'Hallelujah' emanating from the house.

For Wigglesworth, it was as if the Book of Acts had come alive that day: he had acted in faith and God had responded. It now seemed that there was no limit to what he and Polly could achieve through faith and the anointing of the Holy Spirit as they ministered together throughout the country. But Smith Wigglesworth was about to suffer a blow so devastating that it would turn his whole world upside down and, unexpectedly, launch his ministry onto the world stage.

Chapter Five

FIRST AMERICA, THEN THE WORLD

Polly once remarked to Wigglesworth: 'Smith, you watch me when I'm preaching. I get so near to heaven when I'm preaching that some day I'll be off.' It proved to be a prophetic statement, for on New Year's Day 1913, Polly was leaving the Bowland Street Mission after speaking at a meeting when she collapsed and died of heart failure at the mission door. Wigglesworth himself was just leaving the house to board a train for Glasgow, Scotland, when he was met at the front door by a doctor and a policeman who broke the news to him. He stood in stunned silence for what seemed an eternity, for only a few hours before he had kissed his beloved Polly farewell. Then, rather than breaking down and weeping, he began praising God in tongues and laughing in the Spirit, observed by the two bemused onlookers, for he knew she had achieved her most cherished goal – to be with her Lord.

Polly's body was brought back to Victor Road from the mission, followed by a procession of mourners that grew in number as the news of her sudden death travelled like wildfire around Bradford. Soon the house was crammed with people, including the Wigglesworth children, some weeping, others sympathising with Wigglesworth. But he was deaf to their condolences for he had already made up his mind about what he was going to do. On his instructions, she was carried to her room and laid gently on the bed. Wigglesworth closed the door and locked it. Then, with an intensity compounded by his grief, he approached the bed and rebuked the spirit of death in the name of Jesus, and at that very moment Polly's spirit returned to her body and she opened her eyes, blinking.

According to one account, Polly asked him why he had brought her back from the dead and he replied that he needed her desperately. She told him gently that her work on earth was finished and that God wanted her. They talked for a while and then he agreed to allow her to go, at which point she lay down on the pillow and smiled as her spirit departed for the second and final time. Wigglesworth recalled, while preaching a decade later, that God had said to him, 'She is mine, her work is done. She's mine.' It was the ultimate sacrifice, and one can imagine Wigglesworth sitting disconsolate on the edge of the bed next to his beloved wife, weeping uncontrollably, his whole body wracked by his grief-stricken sobs.

'They laid her in her coffin,' recalled Wigglesworth, 'and I brought my sons and daughters into the room and said, "Is she there?"

'They said, "No, Father."

'I said. "We will cover her up." If you go on mourning the loss of loved ones who have gone to be with Christ, I say this in love to you, you have never had the revelation that Paul spoke of when he showed us that it is better to go than to stay.'

Polly was buried at a cemetery in Nabb Wood, Shipley on the outskirts of Bradford. After the funeral Wigglesworth returned and lay on her grave. In 1922, while Wigglesworth was conducting a crusade in New Zealand, he was asked by his host, Harry Roberts, the secret of his great anointing. With tears trickling down his face and in a broken voice, Wigglesworth replied, 'I'm sorry you asked me that question, but I will answer it. I wanted to die there. But God spoke to me and told me to rise up and come away. I told him if he would give me a double portion of the Spirit – my wife's and my own – I would go and preach the gospel. God was gracious to me and answered my request. But I sail the high seas alone. I am a lonely man, and many a time all I can do is to weep and weep.'

Two years later, on 22 March 1915, Wigglesworth was dealt another severe blow when his youngest son, eighteen-year-old George, died, possibly on the battlefields of Flanders. It was a loss that he found very difficult to come to terms with.[1]

Some commented, following this double blow, that Wigglesworth appeared to attain a greater depth of compassion for the lost and the suffering. He was to say himself that, 'God has broken me a thousand times. I have wept. I have travailed many a night till God broke me. It seems that until God has mowed you down, you never can have this long suffering for others.' Another time he remarked, 'God has repeatedly sent His steamroller over me and flattened me out, but He has never left me on the ground.'

Wigglesworth's only daughter, Alice, in many ways took the place of Polly, caring for him and helping him with his correspondence. Alice Wigglesworth (1884–1964) left for the Congo in southern Africa in her early twenties to become a missionary and it was there that she married a Mr Smith in 1911. The marriage, however, was short-lived, her husband dying of disease. In 1919, Alice married James Salter (1890–1972), one of the pioneers, along with William Burton, of the Congo Evangelistic Mission.

The Salters were to become Wigglesworth's regular travelling companions in his later years and would often minister alongside him on the platform.

One day, not long after Polly's death, Wigglesworth announced to his stunned congregation at the Bowland Street Mission that God was directing him to go to Canada and the United States. Wigglesworth responded to the call by laying down certain conditions. 'I said Lord, you have three things to do: you have to find money for home and find money to go, and you have to give me a real change, for you know that sometimes my mind or memory is no good at all to me.'

Almost immediately, money began arriving from various sources and Wigglesworth confidently informed his children that God was indeed sending him to North America. His youngest son George, perturbed at the prospect of losing his father so soon after his mother's death, remonstrated with him saying, 'Father, Mother's gone to heaven and you are leaving us. What shall we do?' At that moment, there was a knock at the door and Wigglesworth told his son to answer it, adding, 'And let the Lord speak to you through this knock at the door whether I have to go or not.' George returned with a letter and his father said, 'Now, George, open the letter and whatever there is in the letter, read it and let that suffice you whether I have to go or not.' George did as he was told and discovered it contained a cheque for twenty-five pounds, which had been posted six weeks earlier. 'What about it, George,' enquired Wigglesworth with a wry smile, and his son replied, 'Father, I won't say anything else.'

The money continued to flow in, but there was still the question of his poor memory. One day, according to Wigglesworth, he was just about to board a ship in Liverpool when he was approached by a man who gave him a blank diary. According to Wigglesworth, at that moment God spoke to him telling him to record everything that happened that month in the book. 'I did so and I had a memory like an encyclopedia,' marvelled Wigglesworth. 'You see, I never learned geography and God sent me all over the world to see it.'

Wigglesworth sailed for Canada on 19 April 1914 and was able to report in June that he had held successful meetings in Montreal and Ottawa and, having crossed the border to the United States, in Rochester, New York. During the summer and autumn, while war raged in Europe, Wigglesworth blazed a trail across North America, travelling as far south as New Mexico, east to Philadelphia, and then north to Toronto and Winnipeg in Canada, before arriving in Los Angeles, California in early October.

While in Los Angeles, Wigglesworth heard about a series of camp meetings in Cazadero, a campsite in the giant redwood forests of northern California, convened by George and Carrie Judd Montgomery. When he arrived, he introduced himself to the Montgomerys, who must have been curious, if not amused, by this rough-hewn Yorkshireman with a barely comprehensible accent, who expressed an impassioned desire to preach at their meetings. They may have had some misgivings about giving the platform to a stranger, but Wigglesworth's association with Alexander Boddy, one of the featured speakers, and Stanley Frodsham would, no doubt, have allayed their concerns.

Frodsham said after Wigglesworth's death that one of his most cherished memories of the camp in 1914 was accompanying Wigglesworth, George Studd, brother of C.T. Studd, one of the 'Cambridge Seven', and another speaker at the camp, each morning at six o'clock for a short walk through the woods. Along the way they would stop underneath the huge, ancient redwoods and pray with voices raised for saints throughout the world.

On the opening night of the camp, after several ministers had preached, the person in charge of the meeting said to Wigglesworth, betraying his lack of expectation, 'Now it's your turn. Are you ready?' Ignoring the disdainful tone of the man's voice, Wigglesworth replied with a smile, 'Always.' He rose from his seat, removed his suit jacket and advanced to the front of the platform. Within minutes he had the audience enthralled by his unique message on faith and the other speakers were unanimous in acknowledging that Wigglesworth was no ordinary minister. Alexander Boddy, who arrived at the camp after Wigglesworth, said of the meetings: 'The scenes at the evening meetings were sometimes almost amazing. The people in this land are so responsive, and when a stirring address was ended they flung themselves on their knees round the platform. The whole meeting seemed to rush to the "altar", general prayer went up all over the gathering, there was strong crying often merging with praise.'

Yet Wigglesworth was confronted with a daunting challenge right from the start. Among the people who attended his first meeting was a man who was completely deaf. As Wigglesworth rose to speak, the man took hold of his chair and sat right in front of the platform beneath the pulpit. The devil taunted Wigglesworth mercilessly, sneering, 'Now you are done.' This went on for three weeks, with the man coming to meeting after meeting. Then in one service, while the congregation was singing, he suddenly became very agitated, looking around wild-eyed, as though he had lost his mind and clasping his hands to his ears. He then darted out of the tent and ran about sixty yards when suddenly, he was to testify later, he heard singing and a voice that said, 'Thy ears are open.' He returned to the meeting and explained to the congregation that when God healed his ears he heard a tremendous cacophony of sound. Assuming a disaster was occurring he had fled the tent.

Leaving Cazadero, Wigglesworth returned to Los Angeles where, according to Frodsham, he fulfilled one of his greatest desires by preaching at the Azusa Street Mission, the birthplace of the Pentecostal revival in America. He also visited the Pisgah Home, a hostel for the poor and destitute in the city established by Dr Finis Yoakum. Yoakum was a controversial figure who turned his back on a lucrative medical practice after miraculously recovering from the effects of a serious accident to become a leading social reformer and advocate of divine healing. While in California, Wigglesworth preached at various Pentecostal assemblies in Los Angeles and Oakland, and it was of these meetings that he wrote to Boddy in November 1914:

> At points, at all places, including Oakland and Los Angeles, the buildings were thickly packed with people eager to hear the Word of God, and one feels now, as never before, that as the Spirit rests upon us they press to hear the Word of God, as is mentioned in Luke 5:1. God help me!
>
> It was common to see, at the end of the meeting, crowds waiting for the ministry of the health in Christ, and, as in the days of the Acts of the Apostles, as one laid hands on the needy, marvellous changes were instantly wrought.
>
> For instance, at Victoria Hall there came a woman pressed down with cancer of the breast. She was anointed with oil, according to God's Word. I laid hands on the cancer, cast out the demon, and the cancer, which had up to then been bleeding, dried up. She received a deep impression through the Spirit that the work had been done, and closely watched the healing process with a lady friend. The cancer began to move

from its seat, and in five days dropped out entirely into the protecting bandage. They were much interested and full of joy, and, looking to the cavity whence the tumour had come, they saw to their amazement and surprise that not one drop of blood had been shed at the separation of the cancer. The cavity was sufficiently large to receive a small cup and they noticed that the sides were of a beautiful reddish hue. During the next two days, while they were watching closely they saw the cavity fill up with flesh and a skin formed over it, so that at last there was only a slight scar. At two meetings this lady, filled with enthusiasm, held in her hand a glass vessel containing the cancer, and declared how great, great things God had done.

There is a point well worth the notice of the readers of your valuable paper. At Oakland, a fine looking young man, a slave to alcohol and nicotine, came along with his wife to see if I could heal him. They stated his case, and I said, 'Yes, I can heal you in Jesus' Name.' I told him to put out his tongue, and I cursed the demon power of alcohol and also cast out the demon power of nicotine. The man knew that he was free. He afterwards became an earnest seeker and within 24 hours was baptised with the Holy Spirit, thus clearly confirming Mark 16:17: 'In my name shall they cast out devils.'

Wigglesworth went on to describe other miracles in both cities adding that at a Los Angeles meeting, 'all descriptions of sickness, lameness, deafness, tumours, cancers, and brokenness of spirit etc., were healed. Truly one could say that the invitation Jesus gave was fulfilled: "Come unto me all ye that labour and are heavy laden and I will give you rest."'

Wigglesworth returned to Britain from New York onboard the ocean liner the *Lusitania* in February 1915 following a convention in Rochester. He shared a cabin with two men, one of whom poured a glass of whisky, drained it, then poured another glass and offered it to him. 'I never touch the stuff,' said Wigglesworth emphatically. Surprised at the rebuff, the man retorted, 'How can you live without it?' 'How could I live with it?' shot back Wigglesworth.

The man, who had inherited a large fortune, then broke down and admitted not only that he was an alcoholic, but that he was dying due to his heavy drinking. He then confided that he was desperate to be delivered from his addiction to alcohol, but, with his head in his hands, he concluded that it was hopeless.

'Say the word and you will be delivered,' challenged Wigglesworth.

The man looked up bemused, 'What do you mean?'

'Say the word – show that you are willing to be delivered and God will deliver you,' repeated Wigglesworth.

But the man just stared at him uncomprehendingly.

'Stand still,' ordered Wigglesworth. He then laid his hands on the man and cursed the demon spirit of alcohol that was destroying him.

Beside himself with joy, the man shrieked, 'I'm free! I'm free! I know I'm free!' He then grabbed hold of his two bottles of whisky and hurled them overboard.

Said Wigglesworth of the epilogue: 'God saved, sobered and healed him. I was preaching all the way across the ocean. He sat beside me at the table. Previous to this he had not been able to eat, but now at every meal he went right through the menu.'

Wigglesworth arrived in Britain in time for his Easter Convention in Bradford, followed by the Whitsuntide Convention of the Pentecostalists. According to Donald Gee: despite the presence of the well-known Welsh evangelists, George and Stephen Jeffreys, 'The outstanding ministry of Mr Wigglesworth was the outstanding feature of the conference.'

Wigglesworth was invited to be chairman of the first Easter Convention in Preston, which was held following the end of the First World War, a duty that he was to perform regularly until his last convention in 1946. The Preston Convention was to become the largest annual gathering of Pentecostals in Britain, attracting thousands and featuring eminent Pentecostal speakers from around the world, and one of the undoubted highlights was Wigglesworth's chairmanship. According to Donald Gee (1891–1966), 'Those who only knew Smith Wigglesworth as a preacher would probably be surprised to learn that as a chairman he excelled in grace and wisdom. In presiding over those packed gatherings, with a somewhat excited crowd from far and near, he never obtruded himself, yet at the same time was ready instantly with a word or action to keep the touch of God upon the multitude . . . The only meeting in which he personally and deliberately ministered himself was Easter Sunday afternoon, which was set aside for the sick.'[2]

One year when Wigglesworth was chairing the convention, one of the speakers, who had just returned from the mission field, became very intense and emotional as he spoke, creating an unbearable atmosphere. As the assembly became ever more uncomfortable, Wigglesworth rose impassively from his seat on the platform, moved just behind the speaker, put his hand on his shoulder and 'whispered' bluntly, 'Sit down, Brother, you're killing yourself and us.' Turning to the congregation, he said, 'We'll sing a hymn while our brother gets quiet.' When the hymn finished, he told the speaker, 'Go on now and go quieter.' According to a fellow minister who witnessed the incident, the man, far from being humiliated, accepted the rebuke and came to see it as an example of Wigglesworth's compassion as well as his strength.

Chapter Six

WIGGLESWORTH THE MAN

'All 'oo believe in prayer, put one 'and up. All 'oo believe in praying aloud, put two 'ands up,' cried Smith Wigglesworth as he stood on the platform. 'Now, everybody stand up and do it and get what your 'eart desires.' Obeying the evangelist's command, the majority of the congregation rose to their feet and began worshipping God and speaking and singing in tongues, although some remained defiantly in their seats, arms crossed and stone-faced. Gazing at the scenes of unrestrained joy below, Wigglesworth began to dance, hopping from one foot to another, his hands raised in worship, tears streaming down his face, before launching, as he did at every meeting that he conducted, into his favourite refrain:

'Honely believe, honely believe,
All things are possible, honely believe.'

The man standing on the platform was 5 foot 8 inches tall, stocky, with an exceptionally strong build. Receding silver-grey hair framed a rugged, firm-chinned face that was distinguished by small, penetrating steel-blue eyes, a rather stubby nose and a full, neatly trimmed moustache. He was immaculately dressed, as always, in a dark grey double-breasted suit, trousers scored by razor-sharp creases, his size six, handmade shoes gleaming like mirrors. In one big, sausage-fingered hand, he clutched a small black Bible.

Not only was Smith Wigglesworth strong physically, he also had extraordinary energy and stamina, as Thomas Barratt, a pastor and friend of Wigglesworth, discovered when he visited Norway in May 1929: 'Mr Wigglesworth needs a couple of interpreters, as his powers of endurance are enormous. It is only the power of the Holy Spirit that can make a man hold out, meeting after meeting, as he does and, of course, humanly speaking, a wonderful vitality and physical strength.' Far from gesticulating wildly, according to friend and fellow minister, William Hacking, Wigglesworth was poised, dignified and reverential when preaching from the pulpit.

Befitting his physical attributes, Wigglesworth possessed a booming, baritone voice, laced with a thick, Yorkshire accent. James Salter became aware of his father-in-law's vocal power when the evangelist sailed for Australia in 1921: 'As the ship left the dock, he lifted his voice repeatedly in a series of hallelujahs with a clarity and volume I have never heard equalled. He startled his fellow passengers and caused the captain on his bridge to remark, "That man has lungs of steel!"'

Once, Wigglesworth attended a performance of Handel's *Messiah* and as the piece climaxed with the 'Hallelujah Chorus', Wigglesworth bellowed 'Hallelujah!' ecstatically on the final note. As the last syllable reverberated throughout the theatre, startled members of the audience turned to stare at Wigglesworth, but he was lost in the joy of the moment. A journalist covering the event for a local newspaper commented in a report published the following day, 'I have never heard such a voice in my life!'

Curiously, Wigglesworth pronounced 'only' as 'honely'. Similarly, he would refer to his daughter Alice as 'our Halice' and conversely his son Harold as ''Arold' and ''e's 'ealed' rather than 'he's healed'.

Wigglesworth's habit of transposing his As and aitches was demonstrated comically when he was holding a meeting in Sacramento, California. While preaching on faith and healing, his pince-nez glasses got caught up in their chain. As he fumbled with his spectacles trying to untangle them, he called out in frustration, 'Halice!' But his daughter, Alice, being almost completely deaf, couldn't hear him. Getting no response, he shouted louder, 'Halice, Halice!' and thus he continued while there was a titter of amusement from the audience that this great man of faith was fumbling with his glasses while pleading for help from his deaf daughter.

More than one Wigglesworth commentator has suggested that he would have been unpleasant to listen to without the anointing of the Holy Spirit. His sentences were often abstract and disjointed and his speech littered with grammatical errors and malapropisms. But what Wigglesworth lacked in grammatical prowess, he made up for in the sheer depth and profundity of his comments. 'Faith is better than feelings and if you have faith you will have all the feelings you can feel'; 'Some people like to read their Bibles in the Hebrew; some like to read it in the Greek; I like to read it in the Holy Spirit'; and 'I am satisfied with the dissatisfaction that never rests until it is satisfied and satisfied again' are cases in point.

It was not unknown for Wigglesworth to create words of his own, not always intentionally. 'He had a habit of coining words when he couldn't find the English one,' recalled the South African evangelist David du Plessis, 'but he never made up one that I couldn't understand.'

A friend and fellow minister recalled the time when Wigglesworth was preaching in his church on Mark 11:23: 'He shall have whatsoever he saith.' He then asked the congregation whether they had begun to 'saith yet?' and then spoke for twenty minutes on 'saithing'. After the service, the friend mentioned to Wigglesworth that his use of the word saith, in this context, was ungrammatical. Wigglesworth was not convinced and when the man persisted in making his point, Wigglesworth replied: 'I don't know much about grammar, but if you can't saith, get down on your knees until you can.'

According to renowned Bible teacher and Wigglesworth contemporary Donald Gee, Wigglesworth had a tendency to become tangled in long, complex sentences. 'Then,' recalled Gee, 'he would relieve our perplexity by speaking angelically in tongues which he always interpreted himself. It was all part of the sermon. Explain it how you will, there were some remarkable flashes of revelation. The preacher himself probably little understood the sheer theological depth and insight of his own words. Wigglesworth was a Pentecostal phenomenon.' Remarkably, when he interpreted his utterances in tongues his grammar was perfect.

Wigglesworth would also astound Bible scholars with his astonishing insight into the interpretation of scripture, despite having no knowledge of Greek or Hebrew, and they would often be heard to exclaim in amazement, 'What kind of a man is this?'

During his early years of ministry, Wigglesworth's temper was, at times, all-consuming and he could blanch white and quiver with rage over even trivial matters. This weakness, together with a natural impatience, was magnified when he spent two years in the spiritual wilderness during the 1880s. Recognising that he was out of the will of God, Wigglesworth fasted and prayed for ten days in

July 1893, leading ultimately to what he described as his sanctification, which he considered to be the baptism of the Spirit at that time.

However, his abrupt, tactless demeanour remained, which tended to give the impression that he was hard and unapproachable. David du Plessis, who first met Wigglesworth in 1936, described him, rather unflatteringly, as an 'explosive, often cantankerous old man'.

But what was perceived as a shocking lack of diplomacy to some, was the absolute, unadulterated truth to Wigglesworth, who fiercely opposed any form of exaggeration. 'We must be people of our word,' he once said. 'People ought to be able to depend upon our word. If there were five baptised we should never say it was packed and had a thousand in it. He is establishing righteousness in our hearts that we shall not exaggerate on any line. I have declared that as long as I live I shall never exaggerate. Exaggeration is lying. What God wants is a people that is full of truth.'

He was, on all occasions, a man of his word and would refuse to make a vow unless he knew he could fulfil it. Once he promised a young man who had just established a church that he would come to his aid if needed. Some time later, the man sent a telegram saying that he did indeed require his help. Wigglesworth travelled at his own expense in the middle of an evangelistic campaign from the west coast of America to the east because he had given his word.

Wigglesworth's bluntness could be breathtaking. Once, a man had the audacity to interrupt him when he was preaching, with a message in tongues. Glaring at him, Wigglesworth shouted, 'Don't you dare interrupt God's message through me. Sit down.' Shamed into silence, the man quickly sat down. On another occasion, when a woman who regularly gave a message in tongues which

Wigglesworth interpreted, gave an utterance, Wigglesworth said gruffly, 'Sit down, woman, that is of the flesh.'

Once, when he was ministering in a city in the United States, on the first night, before he prayed for the sick, Wigglesworth declared, 'I'll only pray for you once; to pray twice is unbelief.' A prominent businessman joined the healing line and Wigglesworth prayed for the man, informing him that he was healed. The second night, the man stepped up to the altar again to receive prayer, against the advice of the pastor of the church who knew Wigglesworth's uncompromising approach to ministry. When the evangelist came to the man, he peered at him closely and enquired, 'Didn't I pray for you last night?' The man affirmed that he had, but explained that he had not been healed. 'You are full of unbelief, get off this platform!' barked Wigglesworth and shoved the man down the platform steps.

His reputation for being rough and uncouth was reinforced by his robust approach to praying for the sick. There were occasions when Wigglesworth would slap, hit or punch the part of the body of the person that was diseased, oblivious of the age or condition of the sufferer. Once, he was staying in the house of a couple while he was ministering in the United States, when a friend of theirs arrived with a stiff neck, his head on one side. When Wigglesworth saw him he said, 'What's up with you?' On being told, he grabbed hold of the man's head, rolled it around repeatedly and commanded the stiffness to leave in the name of Jesus. The man staggered back holding his head, but was completely healed. On a number of occasions, he drove his fist into the stomach of those suffering from stomach ailments, sending them reeling backwards – but all professed to be healed.

What some failed to comprehend was that Wigglesworth's wrath was directed, not at the people he was praying for, but at mankind's most implacable foe, the devil. When asked by a friend why he hit people when he prayed for them, he replied with a smile, 'I don't hit them, I hit the devil.' When the friend told Wigglesworth, puzzled, that he didn't know it was possible to hit the devil, Wigglesworth retorted, 'You're learning.'

Another time Wigglesworth remarked: 'You can't treat the devil lightly. You have to be rough with him. You have to mean business. You must tell him with authority to come out. It's no use telling him a second time, because if you do, he knows you didn't mean it the first time. You have to have enough authority in the name of Jesus to command him to come out. In that name, he must come out.' Significantly, he also added, 'But you have to be in the right place with God to do that.'

Wigglesworth, aware of the criticism levelled at him for being unnecessarily harsh with those who sought his prayers, attempted to explain the rationale behind his approach: 'You might think by the way I went about praying for the sick that I was sometimes unloving and rough, but oh, friends, you have no idea what I see behind the sickness and the one who is afflicted. I am not dealing with the person; I am dealing with the satanic forces that are binding the afflicted. As far as people go, my heart is full of love and compassion for all, but I fail to see how you will ever reach a place where God will be able to use you until you get angry at the devil.'

One man, who witnessed his father being healed of multiple cancerous lumps at a Wigglesworth meeting in Melbourne in 1922, commented: 'Wigglesworth seemed rough and ready, but none ever complained. He was a man's man and completely fearless. But at the same time, he could be gentle. And he never said no to the sick, day or night.'

Wigglesworth was not averse to using the same methods on himself. On one of the occasions that he ministered at Bethshan Tabernacle in Manchester, England, Wigglesworth was suffering from a bad back and asked the minister, John Nelson Parr to pray for him. Parr did so, gently laying his hands on the area of his back that was painful. 'That's no good, John,' thundered Wigglesworth, 'you must thump it out. Come on, pray properly!' Parr did as he was told and prayed again, hitting Wigglesworth hard on the back. Wigglesworth shouted, 'Hallelujah! That's it. It's gone!' As he was to say, 'Shout, "Get thee behind me Satan," and you will have the best time on earth. Whisper it and you won't.'

The name Smith Wigglesworth is synonymous with faith and healing, and the emphasis on these aspects of his ministry tends to obscure the importance that he attached to purity and holiness and his insistence on being spiritually clean. 'The Holy Spirit will come when a man is cleansed,' he would say, and to Wigglesworth, faith, purity and power were inextricably linked.

'Two things will get you to leap out of yourselves into the great promises of God today,' maintained Wigglesworth. 'One is purity and the other is faith, which is kindled more and more by purity.' 'If there is anything in your heart which is in the way of condemnation, you cannot pray the prayer of faith. Purity is vital to faith.' He was also keenly aware that without purity and holiness he could never confront demonic powers with boldness: 'You cannot bind an evil power if there is any evil in you. Unless everything is cast out of you, you cannot cast out evil.'

Wigglesworth's holiness was graphically illustrated when, ministering at Zion City, near Chicago, Illinois, he arranged a prayer meeting for the ministers of the city. When they arrived, he was already in prayer, switching from English to divine tongues. As he continued, the others fell prostrate to the floor on their faces, and remained there for an hour, gripped by the power of God. Wigglesworth was the only one left standing and as he lifted his hands and voice to praise God, a cloud like a radiant mist filled the room.

A similar episode occurred when Wigglesworth first visited New Zealand in 1922. He attended a special prayer meeting at which eleven leading Christians were present. As he began to pray, one by one they left as the power of God filled the room. Harry Roberts, a Pentecostal pastor who accompanied Wigglesworth on his campaign in New Zealand, was unable to attend the meeting, but vowed that if another opportunity arose, he would remain, even if others had to flee the room. Another prayer meeting was indeed arranged, and after a number of others had prayed, Wigglesworth himself began to lift his voice, and amazingly, the exodus began again. 'A Divine influence began to fill the place,' recalled Roberts. 'The room became holy. The power of God began to feel like a heavy weight. With set chin and a definite decision not to budge, the only other one now left in the room [Roberts] hung on and hung on, until the pressure became too great, and he could not stay any longer. With the flood gate of his soul pouring out in a stream of tears, and with uncontrollable sobbing he had to get out or die; and a man who knew God as few do was left alone immersed in an atmosphere that few men could breathe in.'[1]

Those who visited Wigglesworth's house in Bradford described the sense of awe they experienced as they became aware of the presence of God in his home; many described it as like stepping on holy ground. One pastor who often visited Wigglesworth at his home remarked, 'Mr Wigglesworth was so filled with God that his little home in Bradford seemed to be holy ground, and like Moses of old, I wanted to remove the shoes from my feet in an act of reverence.' An evangelist who slept in

Wigglesworth's bed while he was away recalled, 'I verily felt the power of God in that bedroom.'

To many who did not know him well, Smith Wigglesworth appeared stern and austere, exuding a commanding air of authority like a latter-day Elijah, and they approached him with trepidation. Yet, his gruff, granite-like exterior concealed a heart overflowing with tenderness. He loved fellowship and would weep when greeted by his grandchildren after returning from a ministry trip or when he beheld the ravages that sin had inflicted on humanity.

For Wigglesworth, love and compassion for the lost and the suffering were the essential requisites for ministry, not charisma and spellbinding oratory. 'If you preachers lose your compassion,' he once said, 'you can stop preaching, for it won't be any good. You will only be successful as a preacher as you let your heart become filled with the compassion of Jesus.' One man remarked that at times Wigglesworth's compassionate sobs for those in need were so heart-rending that the entire congregation would weep with him. This compassion was vividly demonstrated when he once prayed for a woman (whose friend Esther Horton was a friend of George Stormont) who was too weak to come forward for prayer on the platform:

> I [Horton] took a friend crippled with rheumatoid arthritis to hear Brother Wigglesworth speak. After his message, he called the sick forward for prayer. Because of her crippled condition, my friend was still at the back of the hall when the others who had gone forward had reached the front.
>
> Wigglesworth looked up, saw my friend struggling and called to her to stand still. He said, 'Sister, the trial of your faith is as gold.' Turning to the congregation, he said, 'We don't need to minister to our sister. She's receiving healing now.'

His compassion overflowed in his voice. He wept as he prayed, and the healing virtue of Jesus ministered life to my friend. She didn't need to go to the front of the church for healing, but she ran forward to show that she was healed.[2]

Social and racial distinctions were alien to Smith Wigglesworth and he could deal very severely with anyone who tried to make private claims on his time and attention. Once, when Wigglesworth was preaching at a church in a city in America, he was asked by the pastor to pray for a prominent woman of high social status at her home, convinced that her healing would make considerable impact on the city. Wigglesworth was reluctant to make a special trip to see her, pointing out that he was holding three meetings a day, but the pastor persisted and it was decided that they would stop by at her home on the way to the evening meeting. James Salter recalled:

We drew up at the door, rang the bell, and were ushered into a palatial room. From there, we moved into a very large bedroom. There like an eastern monarch on a throne sat the gorgeously robed lady in a rainbow-coloured pile of lovely embroidered cushions.

Smith Wigglesworth stood and stared at such a sight. Then he said, 'Well! You certainly look comfortable!'

'I beg your pardon,' she snapped.

'I said, "You look very comfortable!"'

She let loose in a storm of abuse which left her exhausted.

'Oh!' he said, 'I can see that you are not ready for me yet. Good evening.' And saying that he walked out of the house and entered the waiting car.

My wife and I followed him out and ventured to suggest that he had been a bit harsh with the lady. 'I know my business,' he said.

The pastors remained in the bedroom for some while in an endeavour to placate the lady. When they came out they pleaded with him to go back and pray with her, but he was adamant, saying, 'No, she is not ready for me. Let us go to the meeting.'[3]

The following morning there was another service and, as was his usual practice, Wigglesworth invited those with needs to come to the platform. He had barely finished speaking, when a woman darted out of her seat and ran towards the platform. But in her haste, she tripped and fell prostrate – it was the wealthy woman who had raged at Wigglesworth the night before. Scrambling to her feet she came forward to the platform and testified that after Wigglesworth had left, she repented and God had healed her. That morning in the service she had given her life to Christ. 'She was a broken woman,' recalled Salter, 'profuse in her apologies. Again we had been wrong in our judgements and God had vindicated Smith Wigglesworth's action.'

Wigglesworth could deal with insincerity just as harshly. Once, when a man challenged him: 'You believe in divine healing, so what are you doing wearing glasses?'

Wigglesworth fired back, 'And what are you doing with that bald head?'

Among the facets of Wigglesworth's remarkable character were his humbleness and humility and he was, according to one who knew him, entirely oblivious of self, desiring only that people should see Christ through him. Said Wigglesworth: 'It is satanic to feel you are different from anybody else, that God has a special message for you, and that you are someone very particular . . . I am to die if I am to cause other people to live. I have to die to what people think about me. You have to die to yourself or you cannot come on to a divine relationship with God.'

And he could be ruthless with those he suspected of employing the platform to promote themselves or their ministry rather than the Lord. 'If you do it outside of Jesus, you do it for yourself,' maintained Wigglesworth. 'If you do it because you want to be someone, it will be a failure. We shall only be able to do well if we do it in the name of Jesus . . . I always know that I cannot be anything for God except when I am nothing. I can only assist another when the principle of death is working in my own life.'

He was often outspoken and could be sharp-tongued, but his humbleness prompted him to seek forgiveness without delay if he felt that he had been offensive. Once, when Donald Gee asked to be excused from remaining at the Preston Easter Convention after Good Friday to speak at another convention, Wigglesworth objected strongly and expressed his displeasure. But, as Gee was to say, 'A little later he humbly asked my forgiveness and apologised in a way that just broke me down.'

Wigglesworth never considered the reaction of others to his statements or actions: fear of man, self-consciousness and embarrassment were emotions that were alien to him. He was at all times, as his friend and fellow minister George Stormont observed, 'totally himself' and allied to his innate boldness was a boldness that came from the Holy Spirit.

His unorthodox methods prompted some to view him as eccentric and undoubtedly he was a unique and highly original individual. A friend described his eccentricities as 'Wigglesworthisms', one such being his habit of singing 'I know the Lord, I know the Lord, I know the Lord has his hand on me,' while holding his Bible on top of his head. One man who travelled with Wigglesworth when he was ministering in Australia in 1922 recalled that when he was ready to retire he would change into an old-fashioned nightshirt and jump into the middle of the bed crying 'Goodnight ,Lord.'

Leon Quest, a minister of the Elim Church in Bradford, who first met Wigglesworth in 1937, as he worshipped at the church on occasions with his daughter Alice, recalled the day when he accompanied the old patriarch on a trip to the countryside: 'Very often at 9 a.m. on a Monday morning there would be a knock at the door of our house. I would hear his voice calling, "Where's that boy?" Off we would go on the bus to Baildon Moor, near the place where he was born and where he worked as a young boy. One morning that I remember we got on the bus and he paid the fare. Often on these journeys he would shout, "Glory!" This day he began to speak in tongues. The conductor asked me, "What's he saying?" I replied, "He's a foreigner!"'

According to William Hacking, Wigglesworth had a keen sense of humour, but was never light or frivolous. Once, when Wigglesworth was in the United States, he stayed with Walter Steelberg, the pastor of Oakland Assemblies of God Church in California, where he was ministering. Steelberg's wife, Ruth, recalled an occasion when they were sitting at the dinner table after a meal. 'The men present were telling amusing incidents from their past and we were having a real good time of fellowship. And Brother Wigglesworth was entering right into it all. Then all of a sudden he said, "It's enough!" He got up from the table and not another word was said. He had got a little caution in his spirit that the conversation was getting out of hand, a little too light. And that was that.'

One day, a number of ministers, including Wigglesworth, were gathered in someone's home and, during a pause in the conversation, one began telling a joke. While the others laughed, Wigglesworth just sat in an armchair impassive and unsmiling. Immediately the minister finished, Wigglesworth, as though he had been oblivious to the joke, raised his right hand and, with eyes closed, prayed a short prayer that created an atmosphere of solemnity and brokenness.

It appears that Wigglesworth had a dry wit that was usually accompanied by a gentle smile and a twinkle in his eye. On one occasion, a young man approached him asking for a promise to stand on. Wigglesworth placed his Bible on the floor and challenged the man, 'Now stand on that.' He obeyed and stood on it and was told, 'Now you are standing on a great heap of promises. Believe every one of them.'

Once, during the 1930s, Wigglesworth was ministering at a convention in Wales. At the end of the convention, a meal was prepared for the ministers who had attended, the centrepiece of which was a roast pig. Wigglesworth was asked to bless the meal and as he rose from his seat, the others closed their eyes and bowed their heads expecting the usual prayer of blessing. 'Lord, if you can bless what you have cursed then bless this stinking pig. Amen,' said Wigglesworth and sat down. There is no record of the reaction of those seated at the table, but one can imagine that they were in a quandary as to whether they should partake of the pig or avoid it.

There were times when Wigglesworth was preaching that he made remarks that may not have been intentionally humorous, but were nonetheless as droll as they were pointed. On a number of occasions, he related an incident that occurred in San Francisco in which he observed a boy writhing in agony on the pavement. Rushing over to find out what was wrong, he discovered that the boy was suffering from severe cramp. Wigglesworth rebuked the affliction and the boy was instantly healed, got up and ran off. 'He didn't even say thank you,' quipped Wigglesworth, much to the amusement of the congregation.

Once he remarked, possibly with a deadpan expression: 'A word about discernment: if you would only practice upon yourself the discernment you think you have, you would have such a revelation of your own selfishness and inability that you would never practice on another the longest day you live.' On another occasion, he asked the rhetorical question: 'When is preaching spoiled? When you go on after you are finished?

Wigglesworth always claimed that from the time he learned to read in his mid- twenties he never read any other book but the Bible. He confided to a friend that because he learned to read so late in life, he felt he couldn't waste time reading other material and he once told his grandson, Leslie, 'If I read the newspaper I come out dirtier than when I went in. If I read the Bible, I come out cleaner than I went in and I like being clean.'

Included in this prohibition were the two collections of his sermons and teachings that were published in his name, but were transcribed stenographically, *Ever Increasing Faith* in 1924 and *Faith that Prevails* in 1938. Presumably, however, he was referring to books in their entirety, for he did admit, while preaching in San Francisco in 1922, that he had read extracts from John Bunyan's *The Pilgrim's Progress* and that they had been a great help to him.

Wigglesworth was, above all, a man of prayer and the Word, and he had unquestioning confidence in the Bible, declaring: 'If a thing is in the Bible it is so; it is not even to be prayed about; it is to be received and acted upon.'

In his early years of ministry, he spent whole nights in prayer, but when he started travelling extensively, he was unable to pray regularly for long periods. But, as he was often to remark, although he rarely prayed for longer than half an hour, he seldom went half an hour without praying. Consequently, he was, particularly in his latter years, in continual, unbroken communion with his heavenly Father, and because he lived so close to God, he was able to perceive people's needs without asking. Even when travelling by car he could often be heard to be murmuring, 'Lovely Jesus'.

At home with his family or even in the company of others, if he felt a prompting from the Holy Spirit he would quietly excuse himself and withdraw to a quiet place to seek the Lord's presence. One friend and fellow minister recalled his walks with Wigglesworth, during which the old patriarch would stop at regular intervals along the way, lift his head up and pray a short prayer before continuing.

'If you find me on the street or anywhere else, if I am alone, I will be talking to God,' said Wigglesworth. 'I make it my business to talk to God all the time. If I wake in the night, I make it my business to pray, and I believe that's the reason that God keeps me right, always right, always ready.'

Mealtimes were always a time for worship, Bible study and prayer. Wigglesworth would start by singing a chorus, followed by a prayer of blessing on the food, a 'bit from the Book' and his commentary on it. Between courses there would be more prayer and the Word, then after the meal, out would come his Bible again and typically he would say, 'Well, we have fed our bodies, now we must feed our souls.'

Smith Wigglesworth had a passion for souls that never dimmed throughout his life, a fervour that flowed from his love for God, and by extension, for humanity. Everything he did in his miraculous ministry, recalled James Salter, was geared towards winning souls for Christ. 'Healing of the body is not the main thing,' Wigglesworth would often say. 'I would rather have one soul saved than ten thousand healed.'

He never missed an opportunity to preach about his Lord, and from the time he gave up working as a plumber up to the very day he died, his life was one of non-stop ministry. James Salter said, following his death: 'To his dying day, he lived for this one thing, rarely coming home – morning, noon or night – but that he had led someone to the Lord or ministered healing to a needy person.'

His ministry even extended to ships, trains and other forms of transport. 'When I'm travelling by train and people know I am on that train and it stops at a station even for five minutes, I'll go to the window and they will say, "Have you got a word from the Lord?" Of course I've got a word from the Lord. The child of God always has a word from the Lord. You've got to be ready. You can't run away and get ready. You've got to always be ready.'

One day, Wigglesworth boarded a train and sat down opposite the only other person in the carriage. Looking out of the window and failing to recognise the passing landscape, he assumed that he had got on the wrong train. When he asked the man where he was going he replied, 'South Wales.'

'Well, if I am wrong I am right. I have never once been wrong in my life only when I have been right,' said Wigglesworth. Gazing at the man, Wigglesworth then enquired pointedly, 'What is the Lord Jesus Christ to you? He is my personal friend and Saviour.' Wigglesworth recounts: 'He [the man] replied, "I do not thank you to speak to me of such things." The train stopped and I said to the porter, "Am I right for Bournemouth? How many stops?" He said three. I said to the man, "It has to be settled before I leave the train; you are going to hell." That man wished he had never met me. The train stopped and I had to get out. I said, "What are you going to do?" He answered, "I will make Him my own."'

Wigglesworth was travelling by train to Cardiff in South Wales one day and sat praying quietly, but did not feel the leading of the Spirit to witness to the people with whom he shared the carriage. As the train was nearing the station, he went to the lavatory to wash his hands, and while there he prayed for a few moments. 'As I returned, I believe the Spirit of the Lord was so heavily upon me that my face must have shone. (No man can tell himself when the Spirit transforms his very countenance). There were two clerical gentlemen sitting together and as I got into the carriage again, one of them cried out, "Sir, you convince me of my sin," and fell on his knees there and then. Soon the whole carriage of people was crying out the same way. They said "Who are you? What are you? You convince us all of sin." It was a good opportunity that God had given me and you can be sure that I made the best of it. Many souls were born into the kingdom of God in that railway carriage.' Wigglesworth claimed that such an incident occurred numerous times during his life.

On one occasion, James Salter accompanied his father-in-law to London to a ministry engagement. At the train station, they boarded a bus to take them to the venue and found that there were only two vacant seats: one at the front and one at the rear. Wigglesworth asked Salter to sit in the rear seat while he went to the front. He took out his New Testament, rose from his seat and said, 'Listen to this.' As the startled passengers stared up at Wigglesworth, he read a passage from his Bible and then began to explain its meaning. 'It made a tremendous impression on those people,' observed Salter. 'Many were weeping. Wigglesworth walked down the aisle laying hands on people and praying for them. Who apart from him would dare to do such a thing on a public transport vehicle!'

Although Wigglesworth witnessed without restraint regardless of the situation, he did not share his faith indiscriminately. Following his baptism by the Holy Spirit, there were occasions when he would say nothing, believing that the anointing that rested on him could convict those with whom he came into contact without any utterance or action on his part.

Wigglesworth, who was friendly with a number of millionaires, could have been a wealthy man, but he eschewed riches, claiming, 'I have a peace no money can buy. I have heaven's smile and that is worth millions of pounds. I have the divine approval that I would not sacrifice for all the gold in the world. A minute under the unction of God is worth more than worlds. The good will of God on my head and heart is priceless treasure. Should I sacrifice these for earth's gold? Never! Never!' At Christmas or on his birthday when friends would ask what kind of present he wanted he would reply, 'There's not a single thing in the world that I want. I have all that I need.'

When Wigglesworth gave up plumbing to minister full time he became dependent on offerings and donations, and was given thousands of pounds during the course of his ministry. But he only kept enough to cover his essential needs and gave the rest away to missions. He took particular delight in giving to the Congo Evangelistic Mission, of which James Salter was the co-founder, and he insisted that at whatever church he preached there should be one or more missionary offerings. For a number of years, he gave all the royalties he received for the book of his sermons, *Ever Increasing Faith*, to missions. He once gave a copy to William Hacking with the stern instruction not to lend the book to anyone else. 'Now Brother Hacking, don't lend this book. It's not for lending. If this book is lent, the folks won't buy it and we want them to buy it. This book has made twenty thousand pounds for missionaries.'

Although he was eager for offerings to be taken for missions, he was strongly opposed to ministers using the pulpit to raise money for themselves. 'You must always be above mentioning a financial matter on your side,' asserted Wigglesworth. 'Always before God in the secret place mention your need, but never bring it to an assembly; if you do, you drop in the estimation of the assembly You are allowed to tell any need belonging to the assembly or the church management, but on a personal line, never refer to yourself on the platform.'

According to James Salter, on one occasion, Wigglesworth went for a walk in a park in London with a millionaire at a time when he had great financial needs. But never once did he mention them to his friend, even though a mere hint would have had the man reaching willingly for his cheque book.

Yet, the man who disdained the wealth of man refused to skimp when it came to travelling, preferring to travel in comfort where possible. Once when he was criticised for being profligate he thundered, 'I'm not wasting the Lord's money, I'm saving the Lord's servant.' Wigglesworth always insisted on being immaculately dressed in a suit and tie, even at home, and his shoes were handmade. He believed that he should honour God in his appearance, but during the Great Depression, he was accused of being lavish at a time of economic hardship.

Nothing could be further from the truth. Wigglesworth loathed waste and extravagance and, according to James Salter, it was considered prudent at 70 Victor Road to keep the household bills from his scrutiny. If he deemed the price of the food served excessive, he refused to touch it and, invariably, it had to be removed from the table. While he was frugal with himself, he was unfailingly generous to others. Stanley Frodsham recalled one particular act of kindness by Wigglesworth when he was visiting he and his wife at their home in Springfield, Missouri, in the United States:

> He must have noticed that we were somewhat shabbily dressed, our income being small in those days, for he took us downtown and purchased a new suit and hat for me and a new outfit for my wife. He was just overwhelmed with joy at being able to perform this kindness to two people whom he loved, and I remember that in one of the stores, like Joseph, 'he sought where to weep'. He went into one dark corner of the store where he hoped no clerk could see him and there he wiped away the copious tears that were falling from his eyes.[4]

Wigglesworth was touchingly childlike in the delight he took in nature, and he was often heard to say, 'No man gets more out of life than I do. I get more out of a minute than most folks get out of a month.' He took a keen interest in the sights of the countries he visited, among his favourites being Niagara Falls in Canada and the Trummelbach Falls in Switzerland. Gazing at the cascading torrents of water, Wigglesworth would weep, pleading with his Lord, 'Like that, my God, like that in me! Out of my innermost being let there flow, like that, vast, fast rivers of living water.'

He loved to walk in the countryside and once his eldest son, Seth, mentioned to him, 'Father, we have found a young cuckoo in a titlark's nest. It is just by the roadside.' His eyes lighting up with excitement, Wigglesworth quickly donned his overcoat and they drove out to examine the nest. When they found it, he watched fascinated as the cuckoo fledgling opened its mouth each time it heard its mother return with food. Typically, it reminded him of a verse in the Bible, Psalms 81:10: 'Open thy mouth wide, and I will fill it.'

James Salter once spent a day with Wigglesworth in the Yorkshire countryside where he recalled his father-in-law's unrestrained joy at being in the midst of God's creation:

> After ascending a long grade, we emerged into a wonderful stretch of moorland – miles and miles of it. As far as the eye could see, the ground was carpeted with a gorgeous covering of purple heather, just at its fullest and best. The sun shone brilliantly, the birds soared and sang, all nature seemed to be revelling in a holiday mood. The air was like balm and Smith Wigglesworth raised his arms in his characteristic way, threw back his shoulders and began to breathe in deeply as he exclaimed, 'This is wine, this is health, this is life!' An elderly man, who was passing, stopped and looked at these extravagant actions. When Wigglesworth saw him he addressed him saying, 'What a wonderful place to live in this must be. Surely people never die here!' He much enjoyed the answer of the old man, who said, with a twinkle in his eye, 'Only once, Mister, only once!'[5]

Because of his sensitivity to the Holy Spirit, Wigglesworth was always unpredictable, surprising, at times, even those who knew him intimately. This unpredictability could be unnerving as a young Lester Sumrall discovered the first time that he visited Wigglesworth at his home in Bradford. Sumrall knocked on the door and stood waiting in his bowler hat, holding a briefcase in one hand and a newspaper rolled up under the arm of the other. Wigglesworth opened the door and glared at him. Instead of the usual greeting, Wigglesworth enquired accusingly, 'What's that under your arm!'

A nervous Sumrall, replied, 'The morning newspaper, sir.'

'Throw it away, throw it away!' thundered Wigglesworth, to a startled Sumrall, 'You can't come in 'ere with that.'

'Yes, sir,' replied a shaken Sumrall, hastily stuffing the paper in the bushes.

Then, with a grim nod of satisfaction, Wigglesworth said, 'Come in.'

They entered the living room, which had a coal fire blazing in the hearth, and Wigglesworth said, 'I was just reading.' Then he read aloud from the Bible for about half an hour. After he had finished the Bible reading, he said to Sumrall, 'Let's pray,' so they got down on their knees and prayed. When they had finished praying, Wigglesworth laid his hands on Sumrall and prayed God's blessing on him. They got up off their knees and Sumrall assumed that was the end of the period of prayer and Bible study, when Wigglesworth said, 'I want to read you some more,' which he did from the Bible for another half an hour and then said, 'Let's pray again.' They got down on their knees again and while praying, a weary Sumrall thought, 'Lord, what did I get myself into!'

Finally their time of fellowship came to an end and they had a lunch of roast beef and Yorkshire pudding prepared by Wigglesworth's daughter, Alice. When they had finished, Wigglesworth put his napkin down, rose slowly from the table and declared, 'Come back again,' and left the room. A bemused Sumrall assumed this was his cue to leave and bade farewell to Alice, thanking her for her hospitality. Leaving Wigglesworth's house and walking up Victor Road, Sumrall reflected on the almost surreal experience, but before he had walked very far, it became apparent that he had not left empty-handed. 'I realised that I had received something, an anointing. I felt different,' recalled Sumrall.

This was the first of many visits that Lester Sumrall made to 70 Victor Road over the next two years and he and Wigglesworth became good friends. Then, with the outbreak of the Second World War in September 1939, Sumrall, as an American citizen, was ordered to leave Britain for his own safety. He visited Wigglesworth for the last time to inform him of his departure to the United States. It was an encounter that he would never forget.

When Wigglesworth was informed by his young friend that he was leaving for America, he began to weep, then stood up and said, 'I want to bless you.' He laid his hand on Sumrall and drew him close. As he prayed a prayer of blessing on Sumrall, tears coursed down his cheeks, dripping onto the young evangelist's forehead and running down his face. These tears were soon to mingle with Sumrall's own, as he wept as the Holy Spirit came upon him. Then Wigglesworth stared directly at Sumrall, his eyes piercing in their intensity and prophesied: 'I see it! I see revival coming to planet Earth . . . as never before. Untold numbers, I see it. The dead will be raised . . . worldwide.' And then, looking at Sumrall with eyes that bore into his, he declared: 'I will not see it, but you will see it.'

This was the last time that Sumrall ever saw Wigglesworth, and he was to say of him, 'He had a sweetness. It was like a well of water springing up and it was so delicious that I would come again and again to drink.' Curiously, during the two years in which he visited Wigglesworth's house on numerous occasions, Sumrall never saw another person.

Chapter Seven

ONLY BELIEVE

Smith Wigglesworth was once invited to a conference in Cardiff, South Wales, to discuss church unity and harmony, with an emphasis on the need for the Holy Spirit and personal holiness. The conference proceeded, much to the relief of the organisers, without any clashes over doctrinal differences, but Wigglesworth was restless. No mention had yet been made of the baptism of the Spirit and he thought to himself, 'Can I remain criminally silent and not tell this great audience that there is a mighty baptism in the Holy Spirit for everyone of them like that which the disciples received on the day of Pentecost?' Finally, during one meeting, he felt that he could keep silent no longer. When it came time for his turn to speak, he rose from his seat, removed his jacket and stepped onto the platform.

'If I had all you have now before I received *this*, what is this I have received since and in addition to all I had when I had all you have,' began Wigglesworth with a typically convoluted sentence, which may have left some of the delegates scratching their heads in bemusement. 'I was saved among the Methodists when I was about eight years old,' he continued. 'A little later, I was confirmed by a Bishop of the Church of England. Later, I was immersed as a Baptist.[1] I had the grounding in Bible teaching among the Plymouth Brethren. I marched under the Blood and Fire banner of the Salvation Army, learning to win souls in the open air. I received the second blessing of sanctification and a clean heart under the teaching of Reader Harris and the Pentecostal League. I claimed the gift of the Holy Spirit by faith as I waited ten days before the Lord. But in Sunderland in 1907, I knelt before God and had an Acts 2:4 experience. The Holy Spirit came and I spoke with new tongues as did the company in the upper room. That put my experience outside the range of argument, but inside the record of God's Holy Word. God gave me the Holy Spirit as he did to them at the beginning.'

By the time he had finished, a tense atmosphere pervaded the hall and some of the delegates glared accusingly at Wigglesworth. The chairman of the conference, fearing discord, as the murmur of discontent grew more strident, quickly drew the meeting to a close. But Wigglesworth had made his point and, in doing so, acknowledged the influences that had formed his Christian life since his conversion at the age of eight at the Wesleyan chapel in his home village of Menston.

Wigglesworth and his brother were found work by their father at a woollen mill on the outskirts of Bradford and it was here that Wigglesworth became friendly with a co-worker, a steam fitter and member of the Plymouth Brethren. Founded in Plymouth, south-west England, in 1834, the Brethren (now called the Christian Brethren) adhered to a strict, literal interpretation of the Bible and among their core doctrines were the Rapture and the Second Coming of Christ.

The Wigglesworth family moved to Bradford in 1872 and Wigglesworth joined a Methodist church, before being drawn by the aggressive soul-winning and militant

Christianity of the Salvation Army, or Christian Mission as it was known when he first became involved in 1875. Although declining to join the Army as a soldier, Wigglesworth, both in Bradford and when he moved to Liverpool, immersed himself in the movement's activities, including all-night prayer meetings and open-air evangelism. Wigglesworth and his then fiancée, Polly Featherstone, withdrew from the Salvation Army in 1882, but their commitment to soul-winning and street evangelism, when they established a church following their marriage, suggests that the Army had a considerable impact on their ministry.

It appears that Wigglesworth and Polly were influenced during the 1880s and 90s by groups associated with the Holiness Movement, which emerged in the mid-nineteenth century as a reaction to what was perceived as the worldliness of the Methodist Church. Those who came out of the Church to form their own movements were united in their desire to return to the early teachings of John Wesley, particularly his two central doctrines of justification and sanctification, the latter which was viewed as a second work of grace.

An extension of the Holiness Movement was the Keswick Convention, a non-denominational conference first convened in 1875 in the town of Keswick in the Lake District in Cumbria which Smith and Polly Wigglesworth attended regularly. The leaders of Keswick were opposed to the doctrine of the baptism of the Spirit accompanied by speaking in tongues which they viewed as unscriptural, believing the baptism to be a second blessing, or work of grace, subsequent to conversion, resulting in the sanctification of the individual.

One group to emerge from the Holiness Movement with which the Wigglesworths had contact was the Blue Ribbon Army. This group was probably led by Elizabeth

Baxter and her husband, Michael Paget Baxter, a Christian publisher and philanthropist known as 'Prophet Baxter' due to his interest in the prophetic. Another group, which had a more profound influence on Wigglesworth, was the Pentecostal League of Prayer, led by a lawyer, Richard Reader Harris QC. This initially trans-denominational movement had a network of around one hundred and fifty groups, a membership of about seventeen thousand and meeting places called League Centres throughout England, one of which, according to the League's publication, *Tongues of Fire*, was the Bowland Street Mission in Bradford.

Wigglesworth's implacable opposition to the belief that speaking in tongues is evidence of the baptism of the Spirit may have been due to the influence of Harris, who in a booklet published by the League entitled *The Gift of Tongues – A Warning*, stated unequivocally: 'The gift of tongues is not a necessary evidence of the Pentecostal Baptism with the Holy Spirit. The most serious error in connection with the present movement is the claim by many that the gift of tongues is the evidence of what they call Pentecost.' It went on to describe such a doctrine as an attack upon the Body of Christ by the enemy.

Following his baptism by the Holy Spirit, Wigglesworth became as dogmatic about the Pentecostal experience as he was insistent before he received the baptism and spoke in tongues, that he had been baptised. He often declared emphatically, 'I believe in the baptism of the Holy Ghost with the speaking in other tongues as the Spirit gives utterance.' And to those who denied the Pentecostal experience he would exhort, 'Put down your umbrellas of prejudice and come into the latter rain.'

Wigglesworth was a hundred per cent Pentecostal, but he never denied the significance of his earlier experience of sanctification and how fundamental it was to his personal spiritual growth. He also maintained a balanced approach to ministry and rejected extremism, particularly an overemphasis on one particular doctrine. While conducting a series of lectures at a Bible college in the United States, Wigglesworth gave this advice to the students:

Don't go mad on preaching only on the baptism of the Holy Ghost. You will be lopsided!

Don't go mad on preaching water baptism. You will be lopsided!

Don't go mad on preaching healing. You will be lopsided!

There is only one thing that you will never go lopsided on and that is the preaching of salvation. The only power is the Gospel of the kingdom. Men are not saved by baptism, not even by the baptism of the Holy Ghost and especially not by baptism in water. They are saved through the blood and preserved by the blood.

Once during the 1920s, Wigglesworth, accompanied by James Salter, was given a guided tour around some catacombs in Rome by a Roman Catholic priest. The priest kept on insisting that he would make a good Catholic, while Wigglesworth claimed that he was a Catholic but not a Roman Catholic, and indeed he was, in the sense of the word defining the all-embracing Body of Christ.

Throughout his life, Wigglesworth declined to join any denomination and was wary of the divisive nature of denominationalism and sectarianism. This even applied to the Assemblies of God, from which he obtained ministerial credentials in 1924, and he was essentially a layman. 'We must recognise that there is only one body,' said Wigglesworth. 'It seems to me that God would at one time have made such an inroad into all nations on the lines of the truth through the Plymouth Brethren, if they had only recognised that there was more in the body than just the

Plymouth Brethren. You will never gain interest without you see that in every church there will be a nucleus which has as real a God as you have.'

'Fancy people sitting round the table and reckoning that that table is the only table,' said Wigglesworth once when preaching. 'What about hundreds of people I know who are sitting round the table every day and taking the bread and wine? Brother, the body of Christ consists of all who are in Christ.'

Wigglesworth was always being asked what denomination he belonged to and he would often reply play- fully, 'I will give you my credentials. They are right here. I put them down so I could always have them ready. TSEWSA.' When the person enquired, puzzled, what such an acronym stood for, Wigglesworth would reply with a smile, 'The Sect Everywhere Spoken Against.'

Typically, on a Sunday he would join the Salvation Army at seven o'clock for early morning prayers, then he would often attend Holy Communion at an Anglican church at eight o'clock, followed by the service at Elim Alliance Church with which his own Bowland Street Mission had merged. Wigglesworth took communion daily at home during the week, partaking of the bread and the wine, even if he was on his own.

He held special services for Anglican ministers on three occasions, and was willing to don surplice and cassock if required. One of these was in 1928 when he conducted a series of meetings for the Revd W.H. Stuart-Fox, the vicar of St Saviour's Church in North London, whose son had been healed at a Wigglesworth meeting. The vicar said of the services, which were held in a tent erected in the grounds of his church: 'The great truths so faithfully pro- claimed of a full redemption for body, soul and spirit through the Atonement, came with extraordinary fresh- ness to the hungry crowds which day by day filled the tent till it overflowed. One of the striking features of the mission was the large number of men, old and young, which came forward to confess Christ, while there were many cases of healing.'

Smith Wigglesworth was described by many as the 'Apostle of Faith' and it was an apt sobriquet for Wigglesworth's faith was indeed colossal. But it would be easy to forget that his faith grew over the years, honed by physical, spiritual and emotional trials, including the loss of loved ones. 'How can we have great faith?' was a question he was often asked and he would invariably reply, 'Great faith is the product of great fights. Great testimonies are the outcome of great tests. Great triumphs can only come out of great trials.'

When he first was asked to pray for the sick, he doubted whether he had the faith to believe for their healing and he was convinced that faith had to be nurtured and cultivated. When out for a walk with some young men from a church, he was asked how one could possess great faith. His reply was as typically laconic as it was profound: 'First the blade, then the ear, after that the full corn in the ear,' he said, quoting from Mark 4:28. 'Faith must grow by soil, moisture and exercise.'

Wherever he ministered, Wigglesworth always sought to raise his listeners' level of faith and he often said, 'My first and most important mission to every church is to stir up the people's faith.' 'Fear looks, faith jumps. Faith never fails to obtain its object. If I leave you as I found you, I am not God's channel. I am not here to entertain you, but to bring you to the place where you can laugh at the impossible.' And critical to building faith, he stressed, was to put faith into action. 'The Acts of the Apostles,' he remarked on a number of occasions, 'is called the Acts of the Apostles because the Apostles acted. God has no room for the man that looks back, thinks back and acts back. If you act with what you have, your faith will be increased. You can never increase faith but by acting.'

His was a faith deeply rooted in the Word of God which he loved and whose authority he had absolute confidence in and never questioned. At the very least, he would always carry his New Testament with him and even offered a reward of five pounds to anyone who found him without his Bible. 'I believe in the Book from cover to cover, as the inspired Word of God,' he would often remark, and a friend claimed that he seldom went more than fifteen minutes without reading his Bible.

Faith was one of his favourite sermon topics and he had much to say on the subject:

Faith cometh by hearing and hearing by the Word of God – not by reading commentaries. Faith is the principle of the Word of God. The Holy Spirit, who inspired the Word is called the Spirit of truth; and as we receive with meekness the engrafted Word, faith springs up in our hearts; faith in the sacrifice of Calvary; faith in the shed blood of Jesus; faith in the fact that He took our weaknesses upon Himself, that He has borne our sicknesses and carried our pains, and that He is our life today. The Word of God is living and powerful and in its treasure you will find eternal life. If you will dare to trust this wonderful Lord of life, you will find in Him everything you need.

All lack of faith is due to not feeding on God's Word. You need it every day. Feed on the living Christ of whom this Word is full. As you get taken up with the glorious fact and the wondrous presence of the living Christ, the faith of God will spring up within you. If I am going to know God, I am going to know Him by His Word. I know I shall be in heaven, but I could not build on my feelings that I am going to heaven. I am going to heaven because God's Word says it and I believe God's Word. Faith cometh by hearing and hearing by the Word of Christ.

And he had this to say about the Bible:

> You must be so soaked with the Word of God, you must be
> so filled with it, that you yourself are a living epistle, known
> and read of all men. Believers are strong only as the Word of
> God abides in them. The Word of God is spirit and life to
> those who receive it in simple faith, and it is a vivifier of all
> who own its sway. Know your Book, live it, believe it and
> obey it. Hide God's Word in your heart. It will save your
> soul, quicken your body and illumine your mind. The Word
> of God is full and final, infallible, reliable and up-to-date and
> our attitude towards it must be one of unquestioned obedi-
> ence.

But even Wigglesworth recognised that his faith had limitations, citing the example of renowned Welsh minister
Rees Howells who, during the 1930s, prayed in faith for
finances to build a Bible college in Wales and received
£100,000, a huge sum of money in those days. 'This does
not seem to be my line of faith,' remarked Wigglesworth,
who was in no doubt that his area of faith was healing,
but he would not go as far as to claim that he had a gift:
'It is not for me to claim that I have a gift. If I have it, the
manifestation of it will be the evidence that it is there. It's
not what I claim, but what God does.'

Wigglesworth believed that it was possible to exercise
the gifts of the Spirit without receiving the baptism of the
Spirit, which he did himself in the case of healing. Once,
when preaching in San Francisco, he was asked the question: 'Are the results mentioned in Mark 16:16–18, to
apply only to those who are baptised with the Holy
Spirit?' In reply, Wigglesworth said: 'Thousands of people who have never received the baptism of the Holy
Spirit are very specially led and blessed in healing the
sick. The finest people that ever I knew, who have never

come into the same experience as I am today regarding the baptism of the Holy Spirit, are mightily used with all kinds of sicknesses wonderfully. But they did not have that which is in the sixteenth chapter of Mark. Only baptised believers speak in tongues.' It is interesting to note that he did not attempt to explain the apparent paradox of how one of the gifts described in this chapter, healing, can be exercised but not another, tongues, which is also mentioned.

Throughout his ministry, Wigglesworth was dogged by criticism regarding remarks that he uttered that were considered outrageously presumptuous, if not heretical. Statements such as, 'If you ask God seven times for the same thing, six times are unbelief,' 'If the Spirit does not move me, I move the Spirit,' and 'Never cast out an evil spirit twice. If you do, the devil will laugh at you,' were both controversial and questionable, and indeed his exegesis was challenged by his contemporaries. But it may have been the case that he was just attempting to emphasise his point rather than being literal.

His doctrine in certain respects was also open to debate. He believed that the Spirit of Christ is different from the Holy Spirit, a view now almost universally discarded by Pentecostal teachers. 'When you are born again,' claimed Wigglesworth, 'the Christ Spirit – not the Holy Spirit, but the Christ Spirit – comes and quickens your human spirit and becomes a new generating power in you, and you are born into a new order by the Spirit of Christ.'

More mainstream, was his belief that there is a difference between the act of speaking in tongues at the time of baptism by the Holy Spirit (described as the initial evidence of the baptism) and the gift of tongues as listed in 1 Corinthians 12. He believed also that without the gift of tongues it might not be possible to speak again in tongues following the Pentecostal baptism, unless under the unction of the Holy Spirit – a doctrine not accepted by the majority of Pentecostals today.

When Wigglesworth arrived home from Sunderland after his baptism, his son George dashed out of the house to greet him and asked excitedly whether Wigglesworth could demonstrate speaking in tongues. But, as Wigglesworth was to say, 'I could say nothing, for although I had received the baptism in the Holy Ghost, I had not received the distinct gift of tongues. That did not come until nine months later. My son did not understand that the speaking with tongues which accompanies the receiving of the baptism in the Spirit is not the "gift of tongues" spoken of in 1 Corinthians 12. The former is given as evidence that the Spirit has come in Pentecostal fullness; but there may not be any further utterance in tongues unless there is a special anointing of the Spirit. The "gift of tongues", however, is such that the receiver may use it for prayer or praise at any time.' And he was to add: 'God gave me the gift of tongues, so that I could speak in tongues any time. But do I? God forbid! Why? Because no man ought to use a gift; but the Holy Ghost uses a gift.'

Wigglesworth contended that the physical manifestations of being filled by the Holy Spirit were a limited, finite experience that ceased after the baptism by the Spirit: 'I only had it once,' recounted Wigglesworth. 'You laugh from inside, and the whole body is so full of the spirit of life from above that you are altogether new. Oh, for God to come into a needy soul and laugh in the soul, it is very wonderful.'

'I maintain that after anyone has received the Holy Ghost, there is no shaking and no falling on the ground. Shaking and falling on the ground is a very limitable position instead of an unlimitable position. There may be a manifestation, but it is not to edification, and the manifestation you are to have is to be to edification. First Corinthians 14:12.'

Smith Wigglesworth's sermons were characterised by their simplicity and rarely did he preach or even quote from the Old Testament, nor from the book of Revelation. According to those who knew him, he usually only carried his New Testament with him, rather than a complete Bible. His favourite and almost only sermon topics were Christ and salvation, the work and gifts of the Holy Spirit, faith and healing. This was possibly his tacit admission that he was no theologian and that he recognised that the Old Testament and Revelation require a deeper, more intimate appreciation of theology and hermeneutics.

A more plausible explanation was his desire to make maximum impact each time he spoke and to convey what he considered to be the fundamental gospel principles of salvation and baptism by the Holy Spirit. 'I am out for men,' declared Wigglesworth. 'It's my business to make everybody hungry, dissatisfied, hungry for God. It's my business to make people either mad or glad. I must have every man filled with the Holy Spirit. I must have a message from heaven that will not leave people as I found them.'

His tendency towards simple, oft-repeated messages may have been a stroke of wisdom on Wigglesworth's part, for his lack of clarity when using Bible terminology brought, on occasion, accusations of heresy. Stanley Frodsham noted that his use of the word 'mortality' led some to assume that he believed that there was no need for a Christian to die, which was not the case at all, for he was to stress that none knew better than he that the 'outward man perisheth'.

Wigglesworth never preached from a prepared sermon, which may have been due to his lack of education and disastrous early attempts to preach, aided by copious notes, at the Bowland Street Mission. He may also have simply preferred to remain spontaneous and guided by the Spirit when preaching. 'I don't come on to this platform with an arrangement of what I have to say,' said Wigglesworth, 'because I have an arrangement with the Father to say what He wants me to say.'

His sermons were generally devoid of structure and were usually short, as witnessed by the brevity of most of the 165 or more of his messages that have been published to date. It was recorded that, once, in New Zealand he preached for an hour and a half, but this was quite exceptional. It was not unusual for Wigglesworth to get dates, names and locations wrong when he related incidents that had occurred during his ministry. This was probably a consequence of an absence of note taking, the sheer number of incidents that had occurred and, as he aged, a failing memory.

Browsing through his sermons, it is difficult to comprehend the sense of awe, excitement and anticipation that must have been present when he preached. They are often rambling and disjointed without any clear focal points. As one person commented: 'There is so much in the man's [Wigglesworth's] personality, utterances in tongues, the choruses that he prefaces and interjects in the course of his remarks, the atmosphere of the meeting etc., that is impossible to convey in a written report.' Unique among Pentecostal preachers of the period, and rare even today, Wigglesworth interspersed his sermons with messages in tongues, followed immediately by his own interpretation.

Wigglesworth preached at Aimee Semple McPherson's Angelus Temple in Los Angeles in the summer of 1927, and she invited him to conduct a series of lectures for students at her Bible college that included some fascinating question and answer sessions. The Bible studies, of which there were twenty-six, lasted for six weeks, during which the students were permitted to ask Wigglesworth anything they liked during the sessions. There is no evidence that Wigglesworth knew in advance what questions would be fired at him, nor that he prepared notes beforehand. His replies to questions – and he never appeared to be lost for one – demonstrated a depth of knowledge and wisdom that was quite extraordinary for a man without any formal education. He also revealed his shrewdness, refusing to be drawn into offering a definitive answer when a student tried to pin him down on a question concerning the salvation of apparent backsliders:

Student: 'I know a number of people who have truly belonged to God and the glory has been upon them, but today they are serving the devil just as faithfully as they ever served the Lord. They have lost eternal life, have they not?'
Wigglesworth: 'You are not responsible for them. They have had the light. Light has come to the world and they refused light. They are in awful jeopardy and darkness and sorrow. If you do not allow God to be greater than your heart, you will be in trouble about them.'

Not to be deterred, the unnamed Bible college student pressed Wigglesworth on the subject again.

Student: 'I am not in trouble about them, but I cannot quite catch the thought that they are still saved.'
Wigglesworth: 'I have not told you that they are still saved. I believe they have tasted but they have never been converted. I tell you the reason why: "My sheep follow me", and they are not of the fold if they do not follow. Jesus said it . . . If I find people that want me to believe that they belong to God and they are following the devil, I will say, "Well, either the Word or you is a liar." I do not take it for granted that

because a person says he has been saved that he is saved. He is only proving to me he is saved if he follows.'

To dispel any notion that he accepted the Calvinist doctrine of predestination, he quickly added, 'Don't you for a moment believe I am here standing for eternal security. I am trying to help you to see that God's eternal security can be so manifested in your mortal bodies that there could not be a doubt toward Rapture or life or anything. That is what I want the Word of God to make you know, that it is eternal life, it is eternal power.'

On another occasion, Wigglesworth was asked the question, 'Once saved, always saved?' and his answer was as pithy as it was profound: 'You were saved by believing. Keep on believing and you will land.'

Chapter Eight

SIGNS, WONDERS AND MIRACLES

In 1933, Smith Wigglesworth held a series of meetings at the Glad Tidings Tabernacle in San Francisco. Lester Sumrall, later to become a world-renowned figure in the Pentecostal movement, but then a young evangelist, arrived in the city soon after Wigglesworth's departure to conduct evangelistic meetings of his own and was told of a remarkable healing that had taken place.

During a Sunday afternoon service at the church, a man on a hospital trolley was wheeled in accompanied by his doctor. The man had stomach cancer and was near death. When it came time for Wigglesworth to pray for the sick, he was brought up on the trolley to the platform. When Wigglesworth got to the man in the healing line he asked his doctor, 'What's up?' The doctor explained that the man was dying of cancer. Wigglesworth enquired where the cancer was and when the doctor explained to him the man's condition, he wound up his fist almost showman-like and plunged it forcefully into the man's stomach. The man promptly died and his hands slipped off the trolley and dangled limply at the sides. Panic-stricken, the doctor screamed, 'You've killed him, you've killed him! The family's going to sue you!' Completely unperturbed, Wigglesworth replied calmly, "E's 'ealed,' and moved on to the next person. About ten minutes later, the man came back to life, got off the trolley and walked down the prayer line in his hospital gown with hands raised, praising God. When the man told Wigglesworth that he had been completely healed, Wigglesworth, betraying no surprise, replied simply, 'Well, praise God for it,' and continued praying for people.

Wigglesworth claimed that ninety per cent of diseases were satanic in origin and top of the list, as far as he was concerned, was cancer. 'When you deal with a cancer case,' maintained Wigglesworth, 'recognise that it is a living evil spirit that is destroying the body . . . You must never treat a cancer case as anything else but a living evil spirit that is destroying the body. It is one of the worst kinds of evil spirits I know. Not that the devil has anything good – every disease of the devil is bad, either to a lesser or greater degree – but this form of disease is one that you must cast out.' There were many occasions when he did just that.

'I had to pray for a woman in Los Angeles one time who was suffering with cancer and as soon as it was cursed it stopped bleeding. It was dead. The next thing that happened was that the natural body had no room for dead matter. It came out like a great big ball with tens of thousands of fibres. All these fibres had been pressing into the flesh. These evil powers move to get further hold of the system, but the moment they are destroyed their hold is gone.'

Wigglesworth prayed for a man who had cancer of the rectum who was in such agony that he required an injection of morphine at ten-minute intervals, twenty-four hours a day. 'I placed my hand upon him in Jesus' name,' recalled Wigglesworth. 'I said to the nurse, "You go to the other room. God will work a miracle." The Spirit of God came upon me. In the name of Jesus I laid hold of the evil power with hatred in my heart against the power of Satan. While I was praying it burst. I said to the nurse, "Come in." She did not understand, but the man knew God had done it.'

Once, Wigglesworth was ministering in Springfield, Missouri, when a man came forward for prayer who had oral cancer. Wigglesworth announced that he would be healed within a few days. He prayed for him and instantly the pain disappeared. He received a letter from the man saying that one day soon after, he spit out half the cancer and the next day the rest of the tumour, losing a quarter of a pint of blood, but healed of the disease.

His method of praying for people always depended, according to Wigglesworth, on 'what the Father had to say.' Often he would anoint the sick person with olive oil on the basis that oil represented the Holy Spirit, as stated in the Bible in Mark 6:13 and James 5:14. So committed was he to this method of prayer that he designed and had manufactured a leak-proof, celluloid oil bottle that had inscribed on the base, '70 Victor Road, Bradford'. According to his contemporaries, many Pentecostal ministers didn't feel fully equipped for ministry unless they had their 'Wigglesworth oil bottle' with them.

At other times, he would lay hands on the sick, often vigorously, and rebuke and cast out the disease. This occasionally involved greater physical force, including slapping, striking or punching the afflicted part of the person's body. Wigglesworth was often heavily criticised for his roughness in praying for people but he was unrepentant: 'You people that are judging me, please leave your judgement outside, for I obey God. If you are afraid to be touched, don't come to me to pray for you. If you are not prepared to be dealt with as God gives me leadings to deal, keep away. But if you can believe God has me for a purpose, come and I will help you.'

Wigglesworth was, humorously, to describe praying for people individually as 'retail' healing, while mass prayer without contact he dubbed 'wholesale' healing. This was a method he first employed in Sweden in 1921 at a large meeting in a park in Stockholm, when the police prohibited him from laying hands on people.

There were times, however, when he did not feel constrained to pray at all. He would simply announce to the person that they were healed. Some were sceptical and would return to the following meeting and join the healing line seeking additional prayer, but they did so at their peril. A man with diabetes joined the healing line at one meeting, but Wigglesworth neither prayed nor laid hands on him but said, 'Go home, you're healed.' Feeling no different, the man came forward again at the following meeting, but when Wigglesworth came to him he looked at him and barked, 'I told you to go home, you are healed.' Shaken, the man obeyed and discovered when he returned home that he was indeed healed.

A reporter from the *Dominion* newspaper attended a Wigglesworth meeting at Wellington Town Hall, New Zealand in May 1922 and described, in a fascinatingly detailed account, how he prayed for the sick:

> Mr Wigglesworth descended to the main floor of the hall. There the sick, the halt and the lame, who desired to be cured by Divine faith, were lined up. It was a curious scene. On the one side of the hall, close to the platform, was formed a rough sort of queue by the people who wished to invoke the healing power of the visitor, each holding a card in his or her hand, on which was inscribed the name of the person and the complaint he or she desired to be rid of.

Smith Wigglesworth with his daughter Alice. Courtesy of Roberts Liardon Ministries.

Mary Jane 'Polly' Wigglesworth, née Featherstone.
Courtesy of Roberts Liardon Ministries.

A portrait of Smith Wigglesworth in old age, taken not long before his death in March 1947. Courtesy of Roberts Liardon Ministries.

Wigglesworth praying for a woman at Aimee Semple
McPherson's Angelus Temple in Los Angeles in 1927.
Wigglesworth remarked that he had a greater anointing
to minister there than at any other place in the world.
Courtesy of Roberts Liardon Ministries.

A rare photograph of Wigglesworth, probably taken when he was in his forties at the beginning of the twentieth century. Courtesy of Desmond Cartwright.

A rare photograph of Wigglesworth without his trademark full moustache, taken when he was ministering in New Zealand in 1922.

Wigglesworth with Harry Roberts, a Pentecostal pastor, who accompanied Wigglesworth on his first evangelistic campaign in New Zealand in 1922. Roberts became the first General Superintendent of the Pentecostal Church in New Zealand in 1924.

Speakers at the Fifth International Sunderland Convention in May 1912. Back row (first), Cecil Polhill. Second row (first), Smith Wigglesworth, Stanley Frodsham (fifth) and Revd Alexander Boddy (seventh). First row (fourth) Thomas Barratt.

The Daily Mirror

THE MORNING JOURNAL WITH THE SECOND LARGEST NET SALE.

FRIDAY, MAY 16, 1913

FIVE PENTECOSTALISTS BAPTISED IN THE SEA: WOMAN FALLS PROSTRATE
AFTER HER IMMERSION IN THE ICY WATER.

The front page of the British national tabloid, the *Daily Mirror*, on Friday, 16 May 1913 was devoted to coverage of a public baptismal conducted by Smith Wigglesworth in the sea at Roker in Sunderland. Five converts were baptised by Wigglesworth in water so cold that two women among them almost collapsed from shock. The caption reads: 'While the converts were in the sea those on the beach danced wildly about, waving their arms and singing hymns.'

Mr Wigglesworth, who has a plain, straightforward style, and is a man of middle age, and burly figure, stood there with his coat off ready to do his best.

A card is handed to a lady helper, who reads out the complaint. The lady patient is deaf and dumb. Mr Wigglesworth inserts his fingers lightly in her ears and closing his eyes, says: 'O Lord, let the light of thy life enter this poor woman and cast out the spirit of deafness and dumbness that she may hear and speak! Answer prayer, O Lord!' In the meantime, an assistant has anointed the head of the applicant for relief and he and another keep their hands on her shoulder, muttering prayers the while. Immediately afterwards, Mr Wigglesworth looked the patient in the eyes and shouted: 'Open your mouth! Say "Jesus!"' And to the consternation of the lady's friends, a small voice said weakly, in a far-off tone, 'Jesus!'

With bodily ills, Mr Wigglesworth was more strenuous . . . Cases of bodily neuritis and rheumatism he treated with great vigour. He rubbed ankles and legs praying the while that the Lord would relieve the sufferer, cast out all satanic influences, and flood the person with 'the light of His perfect life'. One old lady was wheeled on in a 'pram'. She had not moved a limb for years it was said, but the healer got to work with wonderful vigour and enthusiasm. He laid his hands on her head, stroked her forehead and eyelids and then passed his hands over her body and legs, praying fervently as he did so. After two minutes of this work, he said: 'Now, move your legs!' And under the rug, the old lady was seen to move her leg an inch or two. 'You will walk down to the meeting tomorrow evening and testify!' said Mr Wigglesworth, as he passed on to the next.

As he moved down the prayer line he came to a man whose broken leg had not healed properly . . . With that he pommelled the big man on crutches, prayed until he perspired and then, as a final touch, he turned up the man's trousers and rubbed the injured part vigorously. 'Now walk away,' he said and the man walked, smiling and confident, without his crutches.[1]

A method employed by Wigglesworth to minister to those whom he could not see in person was to pray over handkerchiefs and anoint them with oil. This he did in accordance with the scripture in Acts 19:11–12: 'And God wrought special miracles by the hands of Paul: So that from his body were brought unto the sick handkerchiefs or aprons, and the diseases departed from them, and the evil spirits went out of them.'

Thousands were healed worldwide who had received prayed-over handkerchiefs from Wigglesworth. 'When the mail arrived at his home,' wrote a friend, 'and the time for the opening of letters came, we all had to stop whatever we were doing and get under the burden. There was nothing rushed or slipshod about his methods of dealing with these pathetic appeals for help. Everybody in the house must join in the prayers and lay hands on the handkerchiefs sent out to the suffering ones. They were treated as though the writers were present in person.'

One man who had been taking aspirin for twenty years to dull the gnawing pain of rheumatism, arthritis, senovitis and sciatica, and had estimated that he had consumed more than fifty thousand aspirins over that period, was healed as soon as he laid the returned handkerchief on his body.

A woman with cancer requested and was sent a prayer cloth from Wigglesworth. When she received it, she placed it underneath her pillow, intending to apply it in the presence of her family. But as she lay on the bed she felt the presence of God from the cloth and was healed of the cancer.

Not long following Wigglesworth's death, a man and his wife and two children approached James Salter after a service and told him that they had written to his father-in-law requesting a handkerchief that he had prayed over. The man suffered from acute appendicitis and his son had a large growth on his neck. When they received a cloth from Wigglesworth, the man applied it to himself and his son and was completely healed of appendicitis and the lump on his son's neck burst and the swelling disappeared.

A prominent individual who, it appears, may have benefited from receiving an anointed prayer cloth was Britain's King George V. He was sent a handkerchief by an Anglican minister's wife who had been given it by Wigglesworth. She received a letter of thanks from the King.

Wigglesworth's audacity would often startle his companions. On a number of occasions he sent forth the challenge, 'The first person in this audience who stands up, whatever his or her sickness, I'll pray for that one and God will heal him or her.'

'How often our hearts have quaked as we have heard him make that bold announcement,' recalled James Salter, 'for there would be cancers, consumptives, people in wheelchairs, others lying on folding beds, twisted, pitiful cases of all kinds of diseases. Secretly we had hoped that one of the simple cases would stand and not one of the far-gone cancer cases or deformed cripples.

'On one occasion we shook in our seats as, in answer to his challenge, a poor, twisted, deformed man, having two sticks for support, struggled to his feet.

'When Brother Wigglesworth saw him, he did not turn a hair. In his characteristic manner he asked, "Now you, what's up with you?" After he had taken stock of the situation, he said, "All right, we will pray for you." He had the whole assembly join with him in prayer, and then, addressing the man, he said, "Now put down your sticks and walk to me." The man fumbled for a time, then he let his sticks fall to the ground and began to shuffle along. "Walk, walk!" Brother Wigglesworth called, and the man stepped out. "Now run," he commanded and the man did so to the amazement and great joy of all who were present, and to our unbounded relief!'

Wigglesworth was conducting a crusade in England when, one night, as he prayed for people who had come forward for prayer, he came to a young man whose throat was swathed in bandages. Typically, Wigglesworth enquired, 'What's up?' in his heavy Yorkshire accent. The man asked in a hoarse whisper whether anything could be done for him. 'Of course He can,' replied Wigglesworth, 'unless He has forgotten how to make voice boxes!' With that, Wigglesworth placed his hands on the man's throat, prayed vigorously, and ordered him to return home and eat a meal of meat and potatoes. When the young man protested that it was an impossibility, Wigglesworth turned him round and gave him a gentle push, saying, 'Go on your way. Do as you are told. Be not faithless, but believing.'

The man returned the following night to testify excitedly that he had indeed gone home and eaten a solid meal without any ill effects. When he had finished, Wigglesworth enquired, 'Then what are you doing with that bandage around your throat?' He explained that it covered a tube through which he had been receiving food daily and that he was going to hospital the next day to have it removed. 'What the Lord has begun, He can complete,' responded Wigglesworth and beckoned the pastor of the church and his assistants to come and observe what he knew would transpire. 'Now watch this for you'll never see the like of it again.' He removed the bandage and gently began drawing the tube out of the man's throat. Giving the tube to the pastor, Wigglesworth placed his thumb and forefinger each side of the hole and pressed inwards. As he did so, the hole closed up.

On another occasion, Wigglesworth was conducting meetings at a sanatorium for tubercular cases in Arizona in the mid-1920s. A young woman with an advanced case of the disease stood when the call for healing was made. 'Stand out in the aisle,' he thundered and she obeyed, gasping for breath, her chest heaving with the effort. 'Now,' he said, 'I am going to pray for you and then you will run around this building.' He prayed and then he thundered, 'Run, woman, run!' She replied weakly, 'But I cannot run. I can scarcely stand.' 'Don't talk back to me,' barked Wigglesworth, 'do as I've said.' When she hesitated still fearful, he jumped down from the platform and urged her to run. He helped her a little and she clung to him until she gathered speed and finally sprinted around the large auditorium. Another woman, whose feet and legs were crippled by sciatica, was ordered to run by Wigglesworth. When she also hesitated, he gave her a little shove. Clinging to him, she took a few steps and together they ran around the building.

A woman approached Wigglesworth and enquired, 'What can you do for me? I have had sixteen operations and have had my eardrums taken out.' Wigglesworth remembered: 'I said, "God has not forgotten how to make eardrums." She was so deaf that I do not think she would have heard a cannon go off. I anointed her and prayed, asking the Lord to replace the eardrums. However, she remained as deaf as it was possible to be afterward, but she saw other people getting healed and rejoicing . . . She came the next night and said, "I have come to believe God tonight." Take care you do not come any other way. I prayed for her again and commanded her ears to be loosed in the name of Jesus. She believed and the moment she believed, she heard. She ran and jumped on a chair and began to preach. Later I let a pin drop and she heard it touch the floor. God can give drums to ears.'

When he was visiting Belfast in Northern Ireland in 1926, he was approached by a man who pleaded that he come and pray for a woman who was dying.

When I got into the room I saw there was no hope, as far as human aid was concerned. The woman was suffering from a tumour and it had sapped her life away. She could not live out one day. I said, 'Do you want to live?' She could not speak. She just moved her finger. I said, 'In the name of Jesus.' And I poured on the oil (Mr Fisher was with me). He said, 'She's gone.' He was scared, I have never seen a man so frightened in my life. He said, 'What shall we do?' O the place of rest by faith. The place beyond all. Without faith one dare not think of the righteousness which is of God. Stand with God. The righteousness of faith has resurrection in it, and moves on resurrection lines.

A little blind girl led me to the bedside. Compassion broke me up for the child's sake. I had said, 'Lift your finger.' You may think what I did was one of the most absurd things to do, but I did it. I reached over into the bed and pulled her out. Carrying the mother across the room, I put her up against the wardrobe. I held her there. I said, 'In the name of Jesus, death come out.' Like a fallen tree, leaf after leaf, her body began moving – upright instead of lifeless. Her feet touched the floor. 'In Jesus' name walk!' I said. She did, back to bed.

I told this story in the Assembly. There was a doctor there. He was sceptical. He saw her. She said, 'It is all true. I was in heaven. I saw countless numbers of people and oh the joy, and the singing, it was lovely, but the face of Jesus lit up everything, and just when I was having a beautiful time, the Lord suddenly pointed to me, without speaking, and I knew I had to go, and the next moment I heard a man say, "Walk, walk in the name of Jesus!"'

What is intriguing about this story is that, as Jack Hywel-Davies[2] has pointed out, there is no mention of the blind girl being healed as well.

One writer claims he knew of at least fourteen occasions when Wigglesworth raised people from the dead, but then proceeds to name two, one of which is not recorded elsewhere. This is quite extraordinary, as Wigglesworth himself only claimed that three people came back to life after he prayed for them (although he probably made this statement during the 1920s). Then there are the healings that could be described as apocryphal. Apocryphal, not in the sense that God could not have performed the miracles, but that there is a complete absence of documentary evidence to suggest that they occurred, and no record of Wigglesworth referring to them in any of his published sermons, or his teachings and other comments. Two examples of such 'healings' stand out.

According to eyewitness accounts, a child of around two years old with deformed feet was brought to the platform during a meeting to be prayed for. Wigglesworth requested that the infant be placed on the platform and then kicked the child into the audience. The child landed on its feet and ran off down the aisle.

The other is the much-quoted case of a clergyman's legs being created. According to a friend, Wigglesworth told him that he once stayed in the home of a Church of England curate who had no legs. While they were sitting together after supper, Wigglesworth declared suddenly, 'Go and get a pair of new shoes in the morning.' The curate thought he was the victim of a cruel joke, but when they retired for the night, God said to him, 'Do as my servant has said.' Brimming with excitement, the curate spent a sleepless night before rising early and setting off for a shoe shop in the town, waiting impatiently outside the door for the shop to open. When the manager arrived and opened up the shop, the curate entered and asked the shop assistant for a pair of shoes. 'Yes, sir,' replied the shop assistant, 'what size and colour would you like?' When the curate hesitated, the assistant looked at his artificial legs and said apologetically, 'I don't think we can help you.'

Recognising the shop assistant's dilemma, the curate replied. 'It's all right young man, but I want a pair of shoes. How about black, size eight?' The assistant went off and returned a few minutes later with the shoes. The curate then took off his artificial legs and put one stump in one of the shoes. Instantly a leg and foot formed. The same thing occurred when he put a shoe on his other stump. The man then walked out of the shop, no doubt praising God ecstatically and leaving the staff gaping in astonishment. According to the friend, Wigglesworth was not at all surprised, for he was expecting the result.

Wigglesworth was always surprised, however, when a miracle did not occur and wanted to know why. But he was not deterred if the healing was not manifested as he prayed. He once declared, somewhat controversially, 'I want everybody to know that Wigglesworth does not believe in partial healings. Then what does Wigglesworth believe? I believe in complete healings. If the healing is not manifested, it is there all the same. It is inactive because of inactive faith, but it is there. God has given it.'

Nevertheless, there were times, when he had no freedom to pray for people. Once, a man who was ill was brought to Wigglesworth for prayer. He took one look at him and said, 'You ought to be in your coffin.' He challenged the man to be ready and, sure enough, within two weeks he was dead.

And not all were healed, as accounts of his meetings in New Zealand and elsewhere suggest. Probably the two most obvious examples of this anomaly were his daughter,

Alice, and Wigglesworth himself. Wigglesworth's sight began to deteriorate when he was in his fifties and he was forced to wear glasses for reading. He was convinced that his failing eyesight was not just attributable to age, but also to his criticism of those that preached healing but wore glasses at the Leeds Healing Home where he used to attend meetings during the 1890s. Admitted Wigglesworth, 'I got such a bitterness in my spirit that God had to settle me along that line – and I believe that I have not yet fully paid the price.'

Curiously, he was often observed placing his pince-nez glasses on his nose to read, and when they fell off, forgetting to replace them, only to continue reading without any difficulty.

Alice suffered from deafness, employing an ear horn at first but becoming completely deaf in later life. When challenged about his daughter's deafness, he was known to reply with a twinkle in his eye, 'It's her lack of faith.' But in reality, it wounded him deeply. His grandson, Leslie Wigglesworth (son of Seth) said, 'You could almost feel the agony. It was something he had to bear. Yet it didn't make any difference to his faith in the Master.' Wigglesworth was known to extend his hands to Alice and pray for her healing, a healing she was never to experience. It was an enigma that was never solved and Wigglesworth was to say himself, 'Who so can explain divine healing can explain God.'

If Smith Wigglesworth was an advocate of divine healing, he was also a down-to-earth, working-class Yorkshireman, who was never hesitant to provide practical advice where it was needed. He applied that to himself concerning the question of trying to get by without wearing glasses. 'I say this: any person who professes to have faith and then gets a large print Bible so that he will not need glasses is a fool. He presents a false impression before the people. He must see that if he wants to carry a Bible that is not huge, his eyesight may require some help or he may not be able to read correctly.' He then went on to cite the case of a woman he advised who was waiting for God to divinely provide her with a new set of teeth:

A woman came up to me one day and I noticed she had no teeth. 'Why,' I said, 'your mouth is very uneven. Your gums have dropped in some places and the old gums are very uneven.'

'Yes,' she said, 'I am trusting the Lord for a new set of teeth.'

'That is very good,' I said. 'How long have you been trusting Him for them?'

'Three years.'

'Look here,' I said, 'I would be like Gideon: I would put the fleece out and I would tell the Lord that I would trust Him to send me teeth in ten days or money to buy a set in ten days, and whichever came first I would believe it was He.

In eight days, ten pounds came to her from a person whom she had never been acquainted with in any way, and it bought her a beautiful set of teeth – and she looked well in them.

A person is prayed for for eyesight and as soon as he is prayed for, he believes, and God stimulates his faith, but his eyesight is about the same. 'What shall I do?' he asks. 'Shall I go away without my glasses?'

'Can you see perfectly?' I ask. 'Do you require help?'

'Yes. If I should go as I go now, I would stumble.'

'Put your glasses on,' I say. 'For when your faith is perfected you will not require any glasses, and when God perfects your faith your glasses will drop off. But as long as you have need, use them.'

You can take that for what you like, but I believe in common sense.

Neither did Wigglesworth oppose the seeking of medical treatment, although he was concerned that people would put their trust in medical science rather than God. During the early 1930s, a doctor informed him that eating eggs could exacerbate the kidney stone condition from which he was suffering. From that day on, he never ate another egg. 'I am not against doctors,' he once said. 'They have a work that no one else in the world has to do. Apart from salvation, they have a great suffering world of trials and sickness and sorrow to help.' But he did add that he felt that doctors should only be paid after they had cured their patients.

He was, however, vehemently opposed to vaccinations, believing the bacteria were harmful. 'I have seen blindness, idiocy and all kinds of evil come from this hideous science,' thundered Wigglesworth. He once cited the case of a nine-year-old girl, claiming that the girl had been possessed by an evil spirit the day of her vaccination. 'I took hold of the child, looked right into her eyes and said, "You evil spirit come out in the name of Jesus." She went to a couch and fell asleep and from that day she was perfect.'

From the time that he was healed of acute appendicitis, if not before, Wigglesworth was keenly aware of satanic activity and was involved in a titanic struggle in the spiritual realm against demonic forces. Satan was as real to him as his Lord and as well as experiencing divine visitation, there were occasions when he came face to face with his foe. Once he awoke suddenly during the night, aware of a cold, evil presence in the room. Peering across the room, as his eyes became accustomed to the gloom, he saw the devil himself standing there. His reaction was astounding by any standards: realising who it was he said, 'It's only you,' then turned over and went back to sleep. This may appear to be an astonishingly nonchalant reaction to what would be to most a terrifying and traumatic experience, but to Wigglesworth, the presence of demonic spirits, if not the devil himself, was a daily reality.

'We should be like torches purifying the very atmosphere wherever we go,' contended Wigglesworth, 'moving back the forces of darkness.' And that is exactly what he became.

Once, Wigglesworth received a letter from the father of a demon-possessed girl. With tears running down his face he handed the letter to Alice who enquired what made it different from the hundreds of letters he received. Without further explanation Wigglesworth replied simply, 'I will have to go,' and put on his coat and left the house. Wigglesworth arrived at the house in London and was taken by the hand to the girl's room by her parents, who wept as they mounted the stairs. They then left Wigglesworth outside the door. Tentatively, he opened the door and was confronted by a shocking sight: before him was a young girl being held down struggling by four men (some accounts state five men), her clothing torn and dishevelled. Wigglesworth entered the room and stared into the girl's eyes, which were rolling around in their sockets. The demon powers that were inhabiting the girl hissed menacingly, 'I know who you are. You can't cast us out; we are many.'

'"Yes," I said, "I know you are many, but my Lord Jesus will cast you out." It was a wonderful moment. It was a moment when He alone could cope with the situation. The power of Satan was so great upon this beautiful girl that in one moment she whirled and broke away from those four strong men. The Spirit of the Lord was wonderfully upon me and I went right up to her and looked into her face. I saw the evil powers there; her very eyes flashed with demon power. "Though you are many," I cried, "I command you to leave at this moment in the name of Jesus!" She instantly began vomiting. During the next hour, she vomited out thirty-seven evil spirits and she named every one of them as they came out. That day she was made perfect and whole. The next morning at ten o'clock, I sat at the table with her at a communion service.'

So intense and so relentless was Wigglesworth's conflict with the powers of darkness that he was well aware that he could never let his guard down, which was one of the reasons why he eschewed worldly forms of entertainment, even books and newspapers. He believed that any form of relaxation, other than being in God's presence, would leave him vulnerable to demonic attack, which for Wigglesworth was a very real experience:

Sometimes I have been shut in for weeks with demon-possessed men and in the middle of the night watches these evil spirits have jumped upon me, but in the midst of it I have held my ground for God and prayed the man right into perfect deliverance.

I am specially reminded of one man. I was shut in for weeks with him, and every time an evil spirit was cast out of him it leaped on me. The last one to be cast out laid hold of me so that I had to deliver myself first before I could deliver anyone else. In this case the evil spirits used to come out of this man and bind me so that I had to stand still. I couldn't move and the man who was possessed would stand and look at me. And as I commanded the evil spirit to leave I would be free again. That man today is perfectly delivered and preaching the gospel. It took someone who would lay hold of God and not let go until the work was completed.

I remember one day walking with a man who was demon-possessed. We were going through a thickly crowded place, and this man became loud and unruly. I boldly faced him and the demons came out of him. However, I wasn't careful and these demons fastened themselves on me right on the street so that I couldn't move.

Sometimes when I am ministering on the platform and the powers of the devil attack me, the people think I am casting demons out of them, but I am casting them out of myself.

In the middle of the night chiefly, sometimes in the middle of the day, these demon powers would come and bite me and handle me terribly rough. But I never gave in. It would dethrone a higher principle if I had to give in.

A friend once recalled a meeting in which Wigglesworth was just about to enter the pulpit when the air was rent by a hideous, demonic scream. Turning around quickly to see who it was, he jumped off the platform and sprinted up the aisle. Seeing Wigglesworth coming, the man got up and bolted in the direction of the door. As Wigglesworth tried to catch up with him, people and chairs went flying. When the man reached the final row of seats, Wigglesworth tackled him and as they fell on the floor he cried, 'Come out you devil in the name of Jesus!' The man was immediately delivered of the demonic presence and accepted Christ as his Saviour.

On another occasion, Wigglesworth mounted the platform to preach but immediately sensed something was wrong:

I shouted, but nothing happened. I took off my jacket, but nothing happened. I asked the Father what was wrong and He showed me a line of people on a bench opposite the door. They were holding hands and I knew at once that they were spiritualists who had come to bind up the meeting.

So I kept on preaching, but I walked off the platform and down the aisle, still preaching. When I got opposite them, I turned, took hold of the end of the bench, lifted it up and said, 'Out you devils!' They slid in a heap by the door, got up and slunk out. They had not come for deliverance, so I didn't cast the devils out of them. I cast them out with the devils in them. We had no more problems that night.[3]

When he was in Kansas City in the United States one time, he was asked to pray for a demon-possessed woman. When he arrived at the woman's home she started to curse him violently and he commanded the demons to depart. As he made his way to the front door, the woman continued to curse and revile him. Turning to confront the woman and the demon spirits that possessed her, he commanded sternly, 'I told you to leave,' and at that moment, the woman was completely delivered.

Wigglesworth once received a telegram to go to the coastal town of Weston-super-Mare in the south-west of England to pray for a raving demoniac:

I arrived at the place and the wife said to me, 'Will you stay with my husband?' I agreed and in the middle of the night, an evil power laid hold of him. It was awful. I put my hand on his head and his hair was like toothpicks standing on end. God gave deliverance. At six o'clock the next morning, I felt that it was necessary that I get out of the house for a short time.

The man saw me going and cried out, 'If you leave me, there is no hope.' But I felt that I had to go. As I left, I saw a woman with a Salvation Army bonnet on and I knew that she was going to their seven o'clock prayer meeting. I said to the captain who was in charge of the meeting when he was about to sing a hymn, 'Captain, don't sing. Let's go to prayer.' He agreed and I prayed my heart out. Then I grabbed my hat and rushed out of the hall. They all thought that they had had a madman in their prayer meeting that morning.

I went down the road, and there was the man I had spent the night with, rushing down toward, the sea without a particle of clothing on, about to drown himself. I cried, 'In the name of Jesus, come out of him!' The man fell full length on the ground, and that evil power went out of him never to return. His wife came rushing after him and the husband was restored to her in a perfect mental condition.

Chapter Nine

OPPOSITION AND CRITICISM

Smith Wigglesworth rose from his seat at the rear of the platform, removed his dark grey, double-breasted suit jacket and strode briskly to the pulpit. Pausing for a moment, his eyes sweeping the serried rows of eager, upturned faces, Wigglesworth announced in his booming, thick Yorkshire-accented voice: 'I want the person with the worst case of sickness in this place to stand up.' James Salter, sitting behind Wigglesworth, bowed his head, not wanting those in the packed auditorium to notice the look of apprehension on his face. Had his father-in-law gone too far this time?

His fears appeared to be confirmed when a woman, deathly pale and limp was helped to her feet by her two female companions and then started to shuffle towards the platform. From the pulpit, Wigglesworth observed the painfully slow procession edge its way up the steps to the platform and come to a halt before him.

After enquiring 'What's up?' brusquely and, on being informed, announcing to the audience that the woman had cancer, Wigglesworth, instead of laying hands vigorously on the woman and rebuking the demon spirit as was his usual practice with cancer cases, unexpectedly commanded the two women to release their desperately ill friend.

Hesitating, surprised by his request, they loosened their grip on the woman, who, her weakened legs unable to support her, collapsed onto the hard wooden floor of the platform.

Undaunted, Wigglesworth ordered the women to lift her up. Straining with the effort, they heaved their helpless, tottering friend back onto her feet. Again, he commanded them to release the woman. Reluctant this time to comply with Wigglesworth's request, but fearful of his wrath if they disobeyed, they let go of her.

As the woman slumped to the floor for a second time with a sickening thud, an angry rumble of disapproval swept through the auditorium. Suddenly a man stood up, face flushed with indignation and cried, 'You callous brute. Leave her alone!' A murmur of agreement and nodding heads revealed that he was not alone. Wigglesworth whirled round to confront his accuser. 'You mind your own business; I know my business,' he thundered harshly. Spluttering angrily, but unable to withstand the force of Wigglesworth's rebuke, the man sat down grudgingly.

Turning back to the two trembling women, his eyes blazing like fiery coals, he again commanded them to release their grip on their friend. 'Do as I say!' he barked as they hesitated. They flinched in fright and let go of the woman. Those in the audience visibly braced themselves for another stomach-churning smack of soft flesh on unyielding wood. Yet, to their astonishment, instead of collapsing the woman stood upright, swaying a little. Then, a gasp of horror rippled across the hall as a brownish-grey mass sprouting scores of tendrils emerged from the woman and dropped onto the platform.

Both Wigglesworth and the woman stared fascinated at the dead tumorous mass. Then the woman suddenly began weeping, her body wracked by her sobs. Wigglesworth lifted his arms and his face to heaven, tears streaming down his cheeks and dripping onto the platform. The shocked silence was suddenly shattered by a spontaneous eruption of praise as people rose from their seats throughout the hall, with hands held aloft. Wigglesworth's accuser stood also, head bowed his eyes welling with tears, forlorn and forgotten among the euphoria.

Throughout the latter years of his ministry, Smith Wigglesworth was severely criticised by those who misunderstood his methods for what they perceived as his unnecessarily harsh and insensitive approach to praying for the sick and afflicted. Others took exception to what they considered his brusque, tactless manner and regarded him as a rather uncouth maverick. Resentment may have existed among the established churches with members of the clergy disdainful of Wigglesworth's lack of education and eloquence and his working-class background, yet envious of his ability to draw huge numbers to his meetings while their congregations dwindled.

In this, Wigglesworth was not alone. Donald Gee in *The Pentecostal Movement* noted that in its early years, the Pentecostal movement was subject to 'intense and bitter opposition', particularly from the established denominations. The irony was that the Pentecostal revival in Britain began in a Church of England church and one of its foremost figures, the Revd Alexander Boddy, remained a staunch Anglican to the end of his life.

Statements such as 'If the Holy Spirit doesn't move me, I move the Spirit', and 'If you ask for anything seven times, six is unbelief', seemed trite, even blasphemous when taken out of context and with no appreciation for Wigglesworth's limited grasp of the English language. One Anglican clergyman who stormed out of a Wigglesworth meeting, appalled at his apparent irreverence, was stopped dead in his tracks by the Holy Spirit who said to him, 'If you don't go back and enter into that prayer and praise, I will cease to bless you.' Not surprisingly, the clergyman hastened back to the meeting and was greatly blessed. Other comments made by Wigglesworth such as 'I had said it, so it must be,' and, 'Well, if I am wrong I am right. I have never once been wrong in my life only when I have been right,' appeared breathtakingly arrogant, but Wigglesworth spoke bluntly and uncompromisingly as he perceived the facts or the situation, without considering how his comments would be interpreted.

According to Stanley Frodsham, 'Doors were opened to him everywhere, but there were many adversaries.' Never more so than in Wigglesworth's home town of Bradford, where, when he first began his healing ministry during the 1890s, he was publicly derided by many he considered friends. Yet, some of those who denounced him in public would secretly request his prayers for healing in private at night under the cover of darkness. One man who came to Wigglesworth's house seeking prayer for healing of a leg riddled with cancer confided to him, 'If people knew that I was coming to your house, they would never let me come. You have a worse name than any man I ever heard of.' Wigglesworth replied bluntly, that if that was his opinion then he should leave immediately, but the man pleaded to be allowed to stay and Wigglesworth prayed for him and within four days his leg was completely healed.

Despite the enthusiastic support of a contingent of the Bowland Street Mission's congregation, it was never a bona fide Pentecostal church and many were not in favour of the Pentecostal experience. Arthur Frodsham, elder brother of Stanley, on a visit to the mission in 1910, reported that although the church had an admirable open-air ministry, 'they are not in sympathy as a body with Pentecost, and personally one feels that they may be a source of weakness in meetings'.

Although Wigglesworth strongly refuted any suggestion of disunity in an editorial, subsequent events suggested that Frodsham's observations were accurate. In
1919, a number of the mission's elders, who opposed
Pentecostalism, exploited his absence on a ministry trip to
wrest control of the church from Wigglesworth and his
supporters and deprive them of the use of the building.
That same year, the mission building was purchased and
turned into a war memorial hall in memory of those from
the parish who had died in the First World War. It was
also the last year that the Bradford Convention was held
at the Bowland Street Mission. Henceforth, it was convened at a Presbyterian church in the city.

Wigglesworth's unorthodox methods exposed him not
only to criticism but also to attempts at blackmail. Stanley
Frodsham recorded one case in which, at the height of a
revival when thousands were receiving healing, an
apparently crippled woman was wheeled into the church.
Wigglesworth prayed for her in his usual vigorous way
and then moved on to the next person. About a week
later, a letter arrived from the woman's lawyer making
financial claims for damages, presumably for injuries
allegedly caused by Wigglesworth. A doctor's certificate
was obtained and legal action threatened. Although the
claim was completely bogus, the money demanded was
paid to avoid Wigglesworth becoming embroiled in a
court case.

When Wigglesworth visited Switzerland in 1920 as part
of a six-month tour of Europe, he was viewed, initially,
with suspicion and distrust by the authorities, who imprisoned him twice for praying for the sick without a licence.
On one of those occasions, while he was in his prison cell
in the police station, an officer came unexpectedly in the
middle of the night, woke him and told him he was free to
go. Expecting Wigglesworth to grab his clothes and leave

hurriedly, the policeman was stunned when he refused to leave until every officer in the station got down on their knees and allowed him to pray for them.

On another occasion, two policemen arrived at the house of the minister with whom Wigglesworth was staying in the town of Godivil with another warrant for his arrest. The minister informed them that Wigglesworth was away, but invited the policemen to accompany him to the house of a woman who lived in the worst slum in the town. A notorious drunk, who had been arrested on numerous occasions for her involvement in alcohol-induced brawls, she had spent long periods in prison and was well known to the police. But when the woman opened the door of her hovel, the officers were amazed at the transformation that had taken place. Gone were the violent behaviour, the torrent of oaths and the disfiguring sores.

The woman explained to the policemen that when Wigglesworth laid hands on her and prayed she had been completely healed of both her insatiable desire for drink and the festering sores. Said the woman, radiant and with eyes shining, 'God saved my soul at that time and from that moment I have not had the slightest desire for liquor.' Visibly moved by the dramatic transformation in the woman, the officers said resolutely, 'We refuse to stop this kind of work. Somebody else will have to arrest this man.' The case against Wigglesworth was subsequently dropped.

Wigglesworth encountered problems again when he arrived in Stockholm, Sweden in April 1921. His teaching on healing and water baptism and particularly his praying for the sick in public, aroused strong objections from the Lutheran State Church and members of the Swedish medical profession, who joined forces in opposition against him. As a result, both Wigglesworth and Lewi

Pethrus, at whose church Wigglesworth ministered, were arrested by the police. Wigglesworth was released, but Pethrus was detained for further questioning. 'Was it hypnosis?' probed his police interrogator, who also quizzed Pethrus about Wigglesworth's practice of anointing handkerchiefs with oil and praying over them. Pethrus responded by quoting Acts 19:11–12, 'And God wrought special miracles by the hands of Paul: So that from his body were brought unto the sick handkerchiefs or aprons, and the diseases departed from them'.

After a week's consideration by the police, who referred their report to the medical board, no action was taken against Wigglesworth and Pethrus. But the opponents of Pentecostalism were determined to stymie Wigglesworth's continued ministry in the country. Representatives from the state church, medical authority and the police were granted an audience with the King of Sweden in an attempt to win support for Wigglesworth's expulsion from the country. However, one of the nurses in the King's household had been healed of a problem with her leg during a Wigglesworth meeting and told the King about the miracle. He revealed that he was fully aware of Wigglesworth's activities and expressed his sympathy, advising that he agree to be escorted from the country voluntarily, rather than risk being deported.

Wigglesworth's application for an extension of his visa was denied, and Pethrus commented: 'Although it has not been possible for the authorities to prosecute us for the sake of our meetings – which would have entailed direct religious persecution – a way has thus been found in which to aim a blow at our activities after all. The fact is that Brother Wigglesworth has been, to all intents and purposes, banished.'

Two detectives and two policemen duly accompanied Wigglesworth to the Swedish border, but not before he was granted permission to hold a meeting in a park in Stockholm that attracted more than twenty thousand people.

Wigglesworth was largely ignored by the major tabloids in Britain, with perhaps the one exception being front-page coverage in the *Daily Mirror* in May 1913 of an open-air baptismal conducted by Wigglesworth in the sea at Roker, Sunderland. When he first visited New Zealand in 1922, however, he was often subjected to vociferous criticism from the press, which took a keen interest in his meetings. He escaped the wrath of the newspapers in Wellington where he commenced his crusade, but when he moved to Christchurch on the South Island, the editor of *The Sun* newspaper wrote a sarcastic and scathing report of a Wigglesworth meeting he attended:

> When the missionary atmosphere has been created, the missioner gets to work on the sick and maimed: the process of the laying-on of hands begins. Mr Wigglesworth has not lacked patients. His meetings have been largely attended. But, so far as our investigations have carried us, the sufferers easily outnumber the cures. 'Believe', is the slogan. 'If you have sufficient faith,' shouts the missioner, 'I can make you whole.' So the blind, the halt, the lame, people with minor and people with dreadful major ailments, flock to receive man's ministrations. It would not be true to say that nobody is relieved. There never was a faith healer who could not point to a number of satisfied subjects. But when any mortal professes to make the blind see, or to restore hearing to the chronically deaf, or to dry up deep-rooted cancer, by such means as Mr Wigglesworth employs, he is inviting hard words and harsh criticism. It is the cruellest kind of torture to build up an incurable with the certainty of a cure when there can be no chance of success.

Then the diatribe continued:

> Mr Wigglesworth practically maintains that he can perform miracles; that he is one of the Nazarene's successors. It is unfortunate that he is able to persuade many trusting folk that he really does possess the power of the miraculous. And it is just as unfortunate that he can convince people that, when he fails – when, for instance, the blind he has treated is unable to see – the fault is the patient's, not his. 'You haven't enough faith,' he tells a shrinking sufferer. The charge leaves the practitioner free of reproach. We don't know whether any of these 'cures' are permanent; the point is not important now. But we ask any intelligent person to conceive the acuteness of the reaction on a subject racked by a fell disease who discovers that, in his or her case, the 'treatment' has produced no beneficial results. The sense of sharp disappointment, the poignant disillusionment, cannot fail to worsen the condition of the patient. We have an idea that this aspect does not greatly trouble Mr Wigglesworth. But the afflicted, grasping at any shadow, should be warned. The age of miracles is past. Mr Wigglesworth has not the guise of the inspired miracle worker. He has demonstrated here as elsewhere that he is just an ordinary faith healer, with a knowledge of mob psychology and possibly a measure of personal magnetism above the average. Some of those who have attended the mission in Sydenham have our sympathy.[1]

This report precipitated a flood of letters robustly defending Wigglesworth. But there were some, including the Revd J.J. North, who wrote supporting the editorial:

> I did not see your protest against the attempt to capture Christchurch with miracles publicly worked until yesterday. I should like to associate myself with your protest and to say that anything more unlike the temper of the New Testament

I find it hard to imagine. Very cruel wrong has been done to numbers of innocent sufferers, suffering some of them through prenatal causes, and some through their gallantry in facing the common foe in France. Some have been categorically told that they are suffering through their sins, and some have been told that they are possessed by devils. Several are in an indescribably wretched state of body and mind in consequence of this outrage. I hope that the people of the Sydenham Mission, who have done very faithful work for the city in many ways, will be quick to disassociate themselves from these crude heresies.

When Wigglesworth returned to New Zealand in October 1923 for more meetings he encountered renewed criticism, stirring up, according to the Revd J. E. Worsfold, 'religious, atheistic and spiritistic opposition'.[2] Sermons were preached against speaking in tongues and healing with H. Scott Bennett of the Auckland Rationalist Association delivering a discourse entitled, 'Faith Healing Extraordinary – The Smith Wigglesworth Mission – A Study in Theological Vaudeville.'

The editor of the *New Zealand Baptist* pitched in with an article entitled 'Faith, Healing and the Medical Profession' in which he attacked Wigglesworth, whom he described as 'very illiterate'. Another article appeared in the *Baptist* following the meetings in Auckland written by the Revd Joseph Kemp denouncing speaking in tongues as heresy:

Campaigns of healing have been and are being held in various cities and hundreds of thousands of people have been treated in the meetings. All sorts of propagandists are abroad and not a few display marked skill in playing upon the emotional nature of the people and others with great hypnotic influence fling a spell over the susceptible and unwary. The

many voices we hear claim to be of divine authority and all
speak in the Name of Jesus Christ. One of the most pronounced of these is that of the 'Pentecostal Gift of Tongues
Healing Movement' which has been described as a deliberately cooked up frenzy of religious emotionalism of the most
marked type, abandonment to which does incalculable
harm. Many good people are very perplexed on account of
the claims of this cult, which teaches that another Pentecost
has come with a return to apostolic conditions. Tested by the
Word of God we do not hesitate to declare that the movement stands convicted and condemned. There can no more
be another Pentecost than there can be another Calvary or
another resurrection. Signs and wonders there will be at the
end of the age, but a reading of Matthew 24:24 and II
Thessalonians 2:9 will show whether they are of God.[3]

Wigglesworth was not one to consider the consequences of
his actions and he could be impulsive, as demonstrated
when, in a state of euphoria after being baptised by the
Holy Spirit, he got up off his knees and innocently kissed
Mrs Mary Boddy who had laid on hands and prayed for
him. His impetuosity was to have more serious consequences more than a decade later when he was forced to
resign from the Council of the Pentecostal Missionary
Union (PMU). Founded in 1909, the PMU had among its
leading members the Revd Alexander Boddy, Cecil Polhill
(former China missionary and member of the famous
'Cambridge Seven') and Smith Wigglesworth, who served
on the Union's Ruling Council from 1915 to October 1920.[4]

Wigglesworth's departure was the subject of both controversy and an element of secrecy. A Miss Amphlett,
together with a woman who remained anonymous, wrote
a letter to Polhill alleging that Wigglesworth had expressed to her that he had a 'spiritual affinity' with her, a
sentiment that she flatly rejected. Polhill passed the letter

on to T.H. Mundell, a London solicitor who had been the secretary of the PMU since its inception. Wigglesworth had already expressed his views regarding the matter in a letter to Mundell, complaining that the magnitude of the incident had been wildly exaggerated by his accusers:

> The two women in question had joined together to ruin my work and I thought Bro. Polhill would have settled the matter but not so . . . I have written him a letter that I expect him to read to you. I have not sinned but repent of the foolishness and ask for mercy. God has forgiven me and for months has been witnessing to this . . . I am not yet recovered from my over work . . . I truly am sorry that Mr Polhill should stand with the women against me. I am afraid he is not the strong character I have believed him to be. God bless you. Pray much before you say much for I do trust you my dear brother.

Despite Wigglesworth protesting his innocence, the Council met and decided that a request should be made to him to tender his resignation. On the same day, Polhill wrote to Wigglesworth urging him to resign, adding: 'We think also that you should abstain for a prolonged season from participation in the Lord's public work; and seek to retrieve your position before God and man, by a fairly long period of godly quiet living, so showing works meet for repentance.'

Wigglesworth bowed to the Council's will and resigned. His resignation letter, submitted in November 1920 was typically terse and ungrammatical:

> I wish to resign From the Councel of The P m u.
> *Smith Wigglesworth.*

But he was clearly incensed by Polhill's missive and his suggestion that he should take a break from ministry.

Consequently, his second letter to Mundell had a much harder edge:

> I think Mr Polhill has Steped over the Boundary this time. They [are] making thing[s] appear as if I had Committed Fornication or Adultery. I am Innocent of thease things. I have done and acted folishley & God has Forgiven me. This thing was settled in a Scriptural way and after this at the Church & then with Mr Polhill & he ought to of seen the thing through . . .

Wigglesworth replied to Polhill and sent a copy of the letter to Mundell:

> Bradford is Settled & God will settle all. The Good Hand of God is upon me & I will live it all down. This week God has rebuked the oprest thrue His servant.
>
> I shall go Forward Deer Brother and ask you to be Careful That the Gospel is not hindered thrue you That at this time. To do unto me as you would wish one to do unto you. do not Truble to Send any thing to Sign. I Signed my letter to you that [is] all.

On the other side of the copy he sent to Mundell he added:

> From the Letter From Polhill He Rules [the] PMU & Every one Else. I think he will have trouble Later. **Private**. I Pass through London on Tuesday. I get the train to Paris Victoria Wednesday morning. am thinking of Staying at the Victoria Hotel for the night if you would like an Interview I will see you no one else on Tuesday [26th.] I could be at Liberty After 4 o clack I think. I have one or two things to do.

Mundell replied to Wigglesworth, giving him a report of a Council meeting convened to discuss the issue:

Mr Polhill regretted having to report the resignation of Mr Wigglesworth as a Member of the Council which he read as follows: 'I wish to resign from the PMU Smith Wigglesworth'. Mr Polhill stated that the circumstances (which he thought it would be best not to go into) under which the resignation was made, had been fully considered by him and the Hon. Secretary, and he asked the Council to accept the same and which was thereupon agreed to. Mr Polhill stated Mr Wigglesworth would continue to act in the same friendly manner as hitherto to the Council and to the work of the PMU. No particulars were given to the Council and your resignation was therefore accepted without these being required or gone into. So far as Mr Polhill and I are concerned we think well in the interests of God's Kingdom that the matter should be left entirely now for him to deal with.

Mundell's subsequent comments appear to imply that he believed, along with other members of the Council, that Wigglesworth had not accepted or acknowledged what they considered as the gravity of his transgression:

I need to say how much I regret this severance and much more the circumstances which led to it. God always takes drastic measures in dealing with any unrighteousness and whilst He is prepared and declares that He is Lord God merciful, gracious, long suffering, abundant in goodness and truth keeping mercy for thousands, forgiving iniquity and transgression and sin, He will by no means clear the guilty. Exodus 34:5. I take the latter important clause to mean that wherever a sin has not been truly dealt with and confessed following true repentance that there is still guilt to be dealt with. You may rest assured of my fellowship and prayers which I am offering up daily on your behalf, and notwithstanding anything that has transpired our friendship will continue as before. If you are passing through London at any time I shall always be glad to see you here.

There is no record of Wigglesworth's response to Mundell's comments, but their relationship remained cordial and it was Mundell, in his capacity as a solicitor, who signed documents recognising Wigglesworth's missionary status, thus enabling him to receive a ten per cent discount when travelling by ship. As controversy raged at home, Wigglesworth was blazing a trail across Europe – with signs, wonders and miracles following – at the start of a decade of evangelistic crusades that would take him to the far corners of the globe.

Chapter Ten

CAMPAIGNS OF THE 1920s

During the First World War, Smith Wigglesworth continued to hold the annual Bradford Convention at the
Bowland Street Mission and, despite restrictions on
travel, to minister at churches throughout the country.
Among his ministry engagements in 1917 was a visit to
Belfast in Northern Ireland and early in 1918 he was one
of the speakers at meetings at Westport Hall in the town
of Kilsyth near Glasgow in Scotland, one of the first
Pentecostal assemblies in Britain.

Then in 1920, nearly two years after the end of the war,
Wigglesworth, in response to a flood of invitations from
Pentecostal churches, embarked on a whirlwind tour of
Europe. His first stop was France, where he preached at a
number of Pentecostal assemblies, including the Ruban
Bleu Hotel in Le Havre, a temperance hotel in which a
Pentecostal centre had been established in 1909 by its
owner, Madame Hélène Biolley. He then moved on to
Switzerland, ministering at towns around the edge of
Lake Geneva, including Geneva itself and Lausanne.

Wrote Wigglesworth of the meetings in Geneva, where
three hundred people received salvation: 'I have seen
eyes opened of those born blind, and other marvellous
works done, and crowds quickened. They pressed me to

promise to give most of the year to Switzerland.' In another letter he wrote of more healings:

A young woman was dying of consumption, and her doctors had given her up. I laid hands on her in the name of Jesus, and she knew that the disease had passed away. The girl went to the doctor, who examined her and said, 'Whatever has taken place you have no consumption now.' She replied, 'Doctor, I have been prayed over; can I tell the people I am healed?' And he said, 'Yes, and that I could not heal you.' [She then said to the doctor,] 'If I am to tell will you put it in black and white?' And he gave her a certificate, which I saw. God had healed her.

A man was brought into one of the meetings in a wheel-chair. He could not walk except by the aid of two sticks, and even then his locomotion was very slow. I saw him in that helpless condition, and told him about Jesus. Oh, that wonderful name! Glory to God! They shall call His name Jesus. I placed my hands upon his head and said, 'In the name of Jesus thou art made whole.' This helpless man cried out, 'It is done, it is done, it is done, glory to God, it is done!' And he walked out of the building perfectly healed. The man who brought him in the wheelchair and the children said that, 'Father so-and-so is walking.' Praise the Lord! He is the same yesterday, today and forever.

Other astonishing miracles were recorded. A woman with cancer, which was progressively eating away her face, came up for prayer. 'Look at her,' said Wigglesworth. 'She will be here tomorrow night and you will see what God has done for her.' After prayer, she left the meeting. The following night she returned and the cancer was gone and new skin had formed on her face.

A child was brought to a meeting deathly ill. The doctors believed that the infirmity was neurological in origin, but Wigglesworth discerned that the trouble was with the boy's stomach. As he laid hands on him, he vomited and a worm sixteen inches long emerged from the child's mouth.

At the end of one service in Switzerland, two boys approached Wigglesworth and informed him that there was a blind man who refused to leave until he could see. Jubilant at encountering such faith, Wigglesworth told them, 'This is positively unique. God will do something today for that man.'

'The blind man said he had never seen,' recalled Wigglesworth. 'He was born blind, but because of the Word preached in the afternoon, he was not going home until he could see. If ever I have seen joy, it is when I have a lot of people who will not be satisfied until they get all that they have come for. With great joy, I anointed him and laid hands on his eyes. Immediately, God restored his vision. It was very strange how the man reacted. There were some electric lights. First he counted them; then he counted us. Oh, the ecstatic pleasure that this man experienced every moment because of his sight! It made us all feel like weeping and dancing and shouting. Then he pulled out his watch and said that for years he had been feeling the raised figures on the watch in order to tell the time. But now, he could look at it and tell us the time. Then looking as if he had just awakened from some deep sleep, or some long, strange dream, he realised that he had never seen the faces of his father and mother. He went to the door and rushed out. That night, he was the first person to arrive at the meeting. All the people knew him as the blind man and I had to give him a long time to talk about his new sight.'

At a meeting in Neuchâtel, one of Switzerland's most eminent dentists, Dr Emil Lanz noticed as Wigglesworth preached, his fine set of teeth. Reasoning that it was

unlikely for someone in their sixties to have such immacu-
late teeth he assumed they were false, and was determined
to expose Wigglesworth as a hypocrite for preaching
divine healing when he himself wore dentures. At the end
of the meeting, Lanz approached Wigglesworth and
enquired whether he might examine his teeth. Surprised,
but amused by such an unusual request, Wigglesworth
complied. To Lanz's amazement he discovered that Wigglesworth had the most perfect set of teeth he had ever
seen, and at his death at the age of eighty-seven, he still
had all his own teeth.[1] Lanz was to testify later of the
revival that followed Wiggleworth's meetings in Switzerland during the 1920s, in which hundreds were baptised
by the Holy Spirit.

As was so often the case, Wigglesworth was confronted
by demonic opposition as he ministered in Switzerland. A
young man came to a meeting intent on ridiculing him but
was struck dumb before Wigglesworth cast a demon spirit
out of him. At another meeting, three insane people were
planted in the audience by those who opposed his ministry. When they started ranting and raving, Wigglesworth
commanded the demons in them to be silent and there was
no further trouble.

Wigglesworth remained in Switzerland until 7 February 1921 – before proceeding to Norway and Denmark –
visiting towns and cities in the German-speaking cantons,
including the capital, Bern, where one day he was waiting
in the passport office for his passport to be stamped. 'I
found a lot of people, but I couldn't speak to them, so I
got hold of three men and pulled them unto me. They
stared, but I got them on their knees. Then we prayed,
and the revival began. I couldn't talk to them, but I could
show them the way to talk to Someone else.'

Moving on to Norway, he arrived in the town of Bergen
one morning. Assuming that no one knew he was there,

he asked his friend and interpreter, Thomas Barratt, to take him to the fjords to relax for a few hours, as he was so weary after months of non-stop ministry. When he returned to the town, he and Barratt stood and stared, astonished at the sight before them. The streets surrounding the venue where he was to preach that afternoon were crammed with vehicles of all kinds: little Model T Fords and long limousines honked their horns in unison, while drivers atop horses and carts, gesticulated wildly and stately hansom cabs inched forward, their horses whinnying. The pavement was also packed solid with wheelchairs, jammed wheel-to-wheel – all were united in their determination to get to the entrance of the building.

As Wigglesworth observed the chaotic spectacle, he noticed that many of the cars and carriages were filled with the sick and infirm. Removing his jacket and handing it to Barratt, he began clambering into the stalled vehicles and laying hands on the afflicted. Soon there were shrieks and shouts of amazement as one after another was healed.

That evening, as Wigglesworth was sitting eating dinner with Barratt, the telephone rang. It was someone from the Town Hall where he was scheduled to preach that night. The excited voice at the other end of the line described an incredible scene: the building was already filled to bursting point and thousands more people were milling about outside desperate to gain admission after hearing of the miracles that had occurred earlier that day. The local police were overwhelmed by the size of the crowd and were unable to hold the people back.

Wigglesworth put down his knife and fork, grabbed his jacket and, with Barratt in tow, set off for the Town Hall. When they arrived, they were escorted into the building by two police officers, pushing their way through the heaving mass of humanity to the platform. 'When I got inside that Town Hall,' recalled Wigglesworth, 'I never saw anything so packed! I have seen sardines packed – yet these people couldn't have fallen down if they had wanted to! The Spirit of the Lord was upon me. I began to preach. I have forgotten my subject, but I knew I was eaten up with the zeal of the Lord.'

As Wigglesworth paced back and forth on the platform preaching, he suddenly heard the voice of God: 'If you will believe and ask me, I will give you every soul.' He stopped abruptly in mid-sentence and then continued his sermon until he heard the inner voice again: 'If you will believe and ask me, I will give you every soul.' Wigglesworth hesitated. He knew it was God, but dare he ask for every soul? Unable to make up his mind, he continued preaching. Again the voice came, repeating the message. Wigglesworth stopped and, with his eyes closed, he raised his head to heaven and whispered, 'All right, Lord do it. I ask you, please give me every soul.' At that precise moment, cries for mercy erupted spontaneously, as a wave of supernatural power swept through the hall, convicting sinners and backsliders alike.

As Wigglesworth gazed in wonder at the hundreds of souls on their knees weeping and crying out to God for salvation, rivulets of tears poured unrestrained down his cheeks, soaking his shirt. He was to say later regarding the meeting: 'I believe that God gave me every soul. That is my conception of Pentecost.'

The astonishing scenes in Bergen were repeated in Oslo, where mounted police were required to control the crowd. 'Only by a great squeezing could I get into the hall, assisted by the police officers,' recalled Wigglesworth. 'I ministered for over three hours to the sick after preaching for one and a half. Many coming were helpless. Hundreds were healed. A great pile of crutches and sticks and other helps had been left on the large platform. I ministered openly and the crowds looked on and shouted.

The excitement was wonderful as the blind saw and the lame leaped.'

During one meeting in the Norwegian capital, a man and his son limped into the building, both on crutches. When Wigglesworth prayed for the father, who had been in bed for two years, he dropped his crutches and began walking, shakily at first, and praising God ecstatically. When his son saw this miracle he cried, 'Help me, too,' and after prayer, he too was walking unaided. After the meeting, father and son walked home together telling all of their healing.

Arriving in Stockholm, Sweden, in April 1921, Wigglesworth preached for Lewi Pethrus (1884–1974), friend of Thomas Barratt and pastor of Filidelphia Church, which became, by the 1930s, the largest Pentecostal assembly in the world. But when Wigglesworth arrived for three weeks of ministry, Pethrus' body of Pentecostals had no premises of their own and were required to rent the YMCA and an auditorium. Pethrus, in his memoirs, said of the meetings: 'His [Wigglesworth's] teaching was very simple and confined itself almost entirely to belief in God. Nonetheless, his sermons on the promises of God were strangely convincing. He was sometimes quite drastic in his way of approaching the sick, but he won their confidence and there were many who received both mental and physical help through him.'

Madame Lewini, a former actress turned missionary from Denmark who travelled with Wigglesworth during his time in Denmark and Sweden, recorded that at nearly every meeting, huge crowds were unable to enter the building, waiting for hours outside in the hope that if any left the meeting that they might have a chance of taking their place.

At one meeting, a man, his whole body trembling violently with palsy, was lifted onto the platform, where

Wigglesworth anointed him with oil and laid hands on him. He dropped his crutches and, although he still shook, in faith he took one step and then another until he was able to walk around the platform and then the auditorium.

It was during this meeting that a woman began shrieking. Wigglesworth brusquely ordered her to be quiet, but instead she leapt onto a chair and began to shout even louder, gesticulating wildly and crying, 'I'm healed! I had cancer in my mouth and I was unsaved. But during this meeting as I listened to the Word of God, the Lord has saved me and healed me.' She was beside herself with joy as those who listened to her testimony laughed and wept with her.

Of his meetings in the town of Orebrö, Madame Lewini wrote:

It was wonderful to notice, as the ministry continued, the effect upon the people as the power of the Lord came over them. Some lifted their hands crying, 'I am healed! I am healed!' Some fell on the platform, overpowered by the Spirit and had to be helped down. A young blind girl, as she was ministered to, cried out, 'Oh, how many windows there are in this hall!' During the three weeks the meetings continued, the great chapel was crowded daily, multitudes being healed and many saved. The testimony meetings were wonderful. One said, 'I was deaf; they prayed and Jesus healed me.' Another, 'I had consumption and I am free.'[2]

Early one morning, Wigglesworth was travelling by train in Sweden, when the train stopped at a station and an old woman, leaning heavily on her daughter, hobbled into his carriage. With the aid of her daughter, she lowered herself down onto the seat opposite him, grimacing with pain. Observing the woman's plight, he enquired, through his interpreter, what the matter was. Weeping, the woman explained to him that she had gangrene in one of her legs and was on her way to hospital to have it amputated. When he told her that Jesus could heal her, her face lit up with joy and her eyes sparkled with new-found hope.

Then, just as he was about to pray for her, the train stopped, the carriage door swung open and in came a group of workmen who stood in the centre of the carriage between him and the woman and her daughter. The devil whispered mockingly to Wigglesworth, 'Now you are done.' 'No! My Lord will find a way,' replied Wigglesworth silently. As he spoke, the legs of the workman in front of him parted and Wigglesworth got out of his seat, crouched down and put his hand on the woman's leg. The workman and the others stared down at him in bewilderment as he bellowed in stentorian tones, 'In the name of Jesus, I bind and loose this woman.' The woman cried out, 'I am healed! It's all different now; I felt the power go down my leg.'

When the train stopped at the next station, the woman stood up and started to move towards the door. Startled, her daughter asked her what she was doing. Her mother replied that she was healed and was going home. With that she got out of the train and marched up and down the platform proclaiming, 'I am healed! I am healed!' until the train chugged out of the station.

Wigglesworth's final meeting in Sweden, in Stockholm, proved to be his largest in the country. When Lewi Pethrus and other Pentecostal leaders applied for permission to hold a meeting in a park in the city on Whit Monday, the police, fearing a forward surge of people seeking prayer, allowed it to go ahead on the condition that Wigglesworth promised not to lay hands on people. Wigglesworth agreed, confident that God did not require him to lay hands on anyone to heal them. It was estimated that more than twenty thousand people flooded into the park on the day of the meeting to hear Wigglesworth preach, including a number of government officials to ensure he kept his promise.

Surveying the huge crowd from a platform specially constructed for the meeting, Wigglesworth prayed silently, 'Lord, you know the situation. You have never yet been in a fix where you could not handle the situation. Show me what can be done for this poor and needy people without having hands laid upon them. Show me.' Then the answer came: he was to ask all those seeking healing to raise their hands. Wigglesworth obeyed, announcing, 'All you that would like the power of God to go through you today healing everything, put your hands up.' Thousands of hands shot up all over the park.

Not knowing how to proceed, Wigglesworth again pleaded for God's guidance and was instructed to pray for a woman standing on a rock. Directing the others to put their hands down, he asked the woman to describe her physical problems and she told him that she was in so much pain that she was in danger of collapsing if she did not sit down.

'I said to her, "Lift your hands high." I then said, "In the name of Jesus I rebuke the evil one from your head to your feet, and I believe God has loosed you." Oh how she danced and how she jumped and how she shouted! Then I asked, "Are you free?" She replied, "Yes, perfectly free!"

'That was the first time that God revealed to me that it was a very simple matter for Him to heal without the laying on of my hands. I said to the sick people, "Now each one lay hands on yourself, and when I pray God will heal you."'

Hundreds were healed that day, without him touching anyone, and those who accepted Christ as their Saviour were among the seven thousand who received salvation during Wigglesworth's stay in the country. It was also the beginning of what he was to describe humorously as his 'wholesale' healing ministry.

In early 1921, in a little chapel in Henan Province, China, a Danish missionary by the name of Fullerton was kneeling in prayer when, inexplicably, he sensed a strong burden to intercede for New Zealand, a country with which, until then, he had had no association. As he prayed, God revealed to him that a Pentecostal revival was imminent in that nation.

Two years before, while serving with the China Inland Mission (CIM) in Yunnan Province in the south-west of China, he had received the baptism of the Holy Spirit and had spoken in tongues. Dismissed by the CIM, Fullerton moved north to Henan Province, where he toiled among the indigenous population for nearly two years without a single convert. One Sunday night, only four Chinese turned up for the service at the chapel out of curiosity. Disheartened, Fullerton retreated to the vestry, fell on his knees and wept bitterly, 'My Lord, two years labour and not a single soul!'

Composing himself, he rose from his knees and returned to the chapel to discover that another man had entered and sat down. After the service, the man approached Fullerton and told him that he had been deeply touched by his words.

The following Sunday, the man brought ten others with him; a week later, forty more came to the chapel; and within a remarkably short period of time, nine thousand Chinese were converted to Christianity and cart-loads of idols had been burnt.

Fullerton returned on furlough to Denmark in the spring of 1921 when Wigglesworth was conducting a series of meetings in Copenhagen. Approaching Wigglesworth after a meeting, he related to the evangelist what

God had revealed to him about New Zealand and asked whether he had ever thought about visiting the country. Wigglesworth had not, but promised to make it the subject of earnest prayer. Returning to Britain, he waited on God for direction and it became clear that it was indeed the Lord's will for him to minister in New Zealand.

He wrote to Fullerton informing him of his decision, and Fullerton and his wife returned to China via Wellington to make arrangements for Wigglesworth's visit to the country. As it transpired, Wigglesworth's arrival in New Zealand was delayed, and Fullerton was compelled to return to China, missing the meetings. Instead, he entrusted their organisation to a Pentecostal pastor, Harry V. Roberts,[3] who had been a regular contributor to his mission in China, and other Christian ministers who were members of a group called the Christian Covenanters.

Coinciding with Wigglesworth's decision to visit New Zealand was the arrival of an invitation to minister in Australia from one of the pioneers of Pentecostalism in the country, Janet Lancaster. Known affectionately as 'Mother' Lancaster, she was leader of the Good News Hall assembly in Melbourne. With the invitation came a cheque for £250, equivalent to an average annual wage then and more than enough to cover his travel expenses. Thus it was that, in late 1921, Smith Wigglesworth set sail for his first crusade in Australia and New Zealand.

As the ship, bound for Sydney via the Suez Canal, slipped its moorings and steamed out to sea, Wigglesworth, true to form, was already planning his own evangelistic campaign onboard. His first step was to announce that he was going to hold a service that coming Sunday, but when he asked whether anyone would come and hear him preach, no one responded. As he was to comment later, 'It was not long before I had plenty of room to myself. If you want a whole seat to yourself just begin to preach Jesus.'

Undaunted, he continued to pray for an opportunity to share his faith and then it came in an unexpected form. He was asked whether he would be willing to participate in an evening's entertainment for the passengers, which was being organised by the ship's entertainment officer. Recalling the incident in detail later, Wigglesworth said that he asked the ship's crew members who had approached him to return in fifteen minutes, giving him time to pray about the matter.

So I had to go quietly to the Lord. 'Can I?' I had the sweetest rest about it. It was all right.

They said, 'What can you do?'

'I can sing,' I said.

Then they said to me, 'Well, we have a very large programme and we would like to put you down and we would like to give you a song.'

'Oh!' I said, 'My song will be given just before I sing. So you cannot put it down until I sing.'

They did not care for that so much, but they passed it on.

They came again to me and said, 'We are very anxious to know what place you would like to be put down in the entertainment.'

'What are you going to have?' I asked. 'How are you going to finish up?'

'Oh!' they said. 'We have all kinds of things.'

There wasn't a thing the devil could arrange, but it was all there.

'Well, how are you going to finish up?' I asked again

'We are going to finish with a dance,' they replied.

'Put me down just before the dance,' I said.

When the day of the entertainment came, Wigglesworth took his seat with the other passengers, many of whom were in evening dress, and waited patiently for his turn to perform, praying silently. Finally, it was announced that the last performance of the evening was to be a song by Mr Wigglesworth of Bradford, Yorkshire.

Wigglesworth stepped up to the platform and gave the pianist his copy of *Redemption Songs*, open at song number 809. When the pianist peered at the words, she realised to her surprise and embarrassment that it was a hymn. Returning the book to him, she spluttered, 'I could never, never play that kind of music.' Unperturbed, Wigglesworth replied, 'Be at peace, young lady, I have the music and words inside.'

Taking hold of the hymn book, Wigglesworth turned to face the audience and began his a cappella solo, his baritone voice booming:

If I could only tell it as I know it.
My Redeemer who has done so much for me;
If I could only tell you how He loves you,
I am sure that you would make Him yours today.

As the other passengers realised it was a hymn, the excited chatter halted abruptly and their smiles vanished. Many started to twitch and fidget with embarrassment, while the ship's crew shot nervous glances at each other. Oblivious to the bewildered stares and muttering of his audience, Wigglesworth, his voice swelling, sang the refrain,

Could I tell it. Could I tell it,
How the sunshine of His presence lights my way,
I would tell it, I would tell it.
And I'm sure that you would make Him yours today.

As he launched into the second and third verses, heads began to drop and eyes welled up with tears.

> If I could tell you how He loves you,
> And if we could through the lonely garden go.
> If I could tell His dying pain and pardon,
> You would worship at His wounded feet I know.
>
> But I can never tell Him as I know Him,
> Human tongue can never tell all love Divine.
> I can only entreat you to accept Him,
> You can know Him only when you make Him thine.

And then came the final refrain, 'Could I tell it? . . . ' And nodding 'I would tell it . . . And I'm sure you would make Him yours today.'

As the echo of the final syllable of the hymn faded, an eerie hush descended on the room, broken only by the sobbing of some of the passengers. The ship's entertainment officer, realising that the mood had changed, announced falteringly and with a nervous laugh that the dance would be postponed to another evening, but no one was listening.

As Wigglesworth stepped off the platform, some voiced their annoyance that he had ruined the atmosphere, complaining angrily, 'You've spoiled it.' One of the clergymen that Wigglesworth had observed entertaining the guests, who was on his way to India to serve as a missionary, confronted him, seething with anger, his face flushed with indignation, 'How dare you sing that song!' he stormed. 'How dare I not sing it,' retorted Wigglesworth calmly. 'It was my opportunity. How could I not tell it?'

Wigglesworth was to discover later that when the clergyman reached India he filed a report back to his missionary society in London saying, 'I did not seem to have any opportunities to preach on board ship. But there was a plumber on board who seemed to have plenty of opportunity to preach to everybody. And he said things to me that I just can't get out of my mind. One thing he said that I can't forget is that the Acts of the Apostles was only written because they acted.'

Following the aborted dance, Wigglesworth had a prayer meeting in his cabin and six young men accepted Jesus Christ as their Saviour. He was to say that from that day on, souls were saved daily for the rest of the voyage, including a prominent Christian Scientist. Responding to an urgent call to come to her first-class cabin, Wigglesworth arrived and announced abruptly, 'I'm not going to speak to you about anything, neither about your sickness or anything. I am simply going to lay my hands on you in the name of Jesus and the moment I do, you will be healed.'

Wigglesworth proceeded to lay his hands on the woman, commanded the sickness to leave and she was completely healed. For the next three days, she wandered the ship's decks deeply troubled, as she pondered her lifestyle and the doctrines she had espoused in England. Finally, in a state of confusion, she approached Wigglesworth for advice.

'What shall I do?' she implored.

'What do you mean?' questioned Wigglesworth.

'For three years I have been preaching all over England,' explained the woman. 'We live in a great house in India and we have a great house in London. I have been preaching Christian Science and now what can I do? You know it is all so real, I'm a new woman. Shall I be able to continue smoking cigarettes?'

Resisting the temptation to share the truth of the gospel with her, Wigglesworth replied to her astonishment, 'Yes, smoke as many as ever you can; smoke night and day, if you can.'

Then she said, 'You know we play cards, bridge and other things. Can I play?'

'Yes, play all through the night, go on playing,' replied Wigglesworth.

Finally, she said, 'You know we have a little wine, just a little with our friends in first class. Shall I give it up?'

'No,' said Wigglesworth, 'drink all you want.'

The woman left, perplexed at receiving such approbation to continue her lifestyle from a man of God. It must have been difficult for Wigglesworth to refrain from sharing about his Lord with the woman, but he had the wisdom to realise that if he had ordered her to renounce her vices, the transformation would be of his own making rather than the work of the Holy Spirit.

By the time the ship steamed through the Suez Canal and stopped at Aden, on the tip of the Arabian Peninsula, the woman had accepted Christ as her Saviour. And she had sent a telegram to Britain cancelling a consignment of a thousand cigarettes, informing her husband, 'My life has changed. I cannot go into these things again.'

While the ship was refuelling and taking on fresh supplies in Aden, merchants came and displayed their wares on the quayside, including carpets, rugs, antiques and trinkets. While Wigglesworth was peering over the side of the ship at the colourful stalls that had suddenly appeared, a man from the first-class deck came up to him and enquired whether he would be willing to join him in buying some ostrich feathers.

'I knew I did not want feathers,' said Wigglesworth, recounting the incident, 'for I had no room or use for them and wouldn't know what to do with them if I got them. But the gentleman put the question to me again, "Will you go shares with me in buying that bunch?" I perceived it was the Spirit as clearly as anything and I said, "Yes, I will." So the feathers were down for three pounds. Then I found the man had no money on him. He had plenty in his cabin. I perceived it was the Spirit again, so it fell to my lot to pay for the feathers. He said to me, "I will get the money and give it to one of the stewards." I replied, "No, that is not business. I am known all over the ship. You seek me out."

The man came and brought the money. I said, "God wants me to talk to you. Now sit down." So he sat down and in ten minutes' time the whole of his life was unhinged, unravelled, broken up, so broken that like a big baby he wept and cried for salvation.'

The ship docked at Bombay, India and then went on to Ceylon (Sri Lanka), where Wigglesworth ministered tirelessly, particularly in the capital, Colombo. In the oppressive tropical heat and with the nauseating stench of filth, unwashed bodies and putrefying wounds, he prayed and laid hands on the sick and dying, weeping with compassion.

Said Wigglesworth:

I was preaching under the anointing of the Spirit and a crowd gathered. They packed the place to suffocation. But the power of God was wonderful. After preaching, and that through an interpreter, in a temperature of about 120 degrees, we prayed for about 500 sick people each night.

In that great heat, women would bring their babies. We would sometimes have fifty or more in the meeting and because the atmosphere was so oppressive they would be crying. I used to say, 'Before I preach I will minister to the babies.' It was wonderful, as soon as hands were laid on these babies, to notice the silence, the quietness, the peace and the order of those meetings! The power of God was there. One man in the midst of the great crowd, who had been blind for a long time, was healed. His eyes were opened instantly. We saw many similar miracles take place.

I cannot understand how God can give to any of His children glory and virtue, but it is, nevertheless, true that He does. There were thousands of people that could not get into the meeting, but as I passed out through the great crowd, people that could not get inside reached out and touched me and they were healed. [According to Stanley Frodsham, scores who stood in Wigglesworth's shadow were also healed.[4]] I marvel at the grace of God that it could take place. There is something about believing in God that makes God willing to pass over a million people just to anoint you. I believe God will always turn out to meet you on a special line if you dare to believe.

I was in one place for only four days and they were disappointed that I could not stay for longer. I said to them, 'Can you have a' meeting early in the morning, at eight o'clock?' They said they would. I said, 'Tell all the mothers who want their babies to be healed to come and all the people over seventy. It would have done you good to see 400 mothers coming in at eight o'clock with their babies and then to see about 150 old people with their white hair, coming to be healed. In those days there were thousands out to hear the Word of God. I believe there were about 3,000 persons crying for mercy at once. It was a great sight.[5]

Wigglesworth arrived in Sydney, New South Wales, in January 1922 and commenced his evangelistic crusade at a Baptist church in the city, which had been arranged by one of its members, Dr R.H. Fallon. The minister of the church, the Revd William Lamb, agreed to have Wigglesworth preach in his church, unaware that he was fervently Pentecostal. Within minutes of him being introduced, Lamb was to discover, to his discomfort, just what kind of a man he had permitted to occupy the pulpit. Scanning those assembled, Wigglesworth spotted a woman in a wheelchair and asked her to come forward. Then he addressed the congregation:

'I want you folks to know that I am going to prophesy in the name of the Lord that this woman is going to walk. If that prophecy does not come to pass, I will never prophesy again. But if it does come to pass, you will know there is a prophet in your midst.'

A stunned silence was followed by a murmuring of shocked whispers. At the back of the platform, the church deacons, bemused and alarmed, glanced at Lamb seeking reassurance, but the minister, grim and tight-lipped avoided their gaze. Dr Fallon, who had recommended Wigglesworth, could only stare, with acute embarrassment, at his shoes.

In the church hall, the atmosphere was taut with tension and excitement as all eyes were riveted on Wigglesworth and the woman, to see if his prophecy would be fulfilled. Gazing intensely at the woman's hopeful, expectant face, Wigglesworth cried, 'In the name of the Lord, be free!' He then reached forward and lifted her bodily out of the chair and commanded, 'Now walk!' The woman replied hesitatingly that she could not. 'God has healed you, now walk!' shouted Wigglesworth brusquely. At that, he gave her a shove and, as she stumbled forward, she began to walk.

While some in the congregation rejoiced at the miracle that had transpired, others sat stone-faced, repulsed by what they perceived to be his uncouth and presumptuous manner. Lamb was undoubtedly one of those and, evidently, they were in a majority, for that was Wigglesworth's first and last meeting at the Baptist church. From there, he was forced to move to another venue in the city, the Australia Hall, where he held meetings for six weeks.

Once, while he was walking back to his hotel in Sydney with a friend, he passed a man bent double and hobbling with a walking stick, the tortured expression on his face revealing the agony he was enduring. Wigglesworth stopped and stared at the man, deciding that he could not ignore his plight. Turning to his friend and nodding in the man's direction, he said, 'There is a man in awful distress and I cannot go farther, I must speak to him.' He then approached the man and said, 'You seem to be in great trouble.' 'Yes,' he replied, 'I am no good and never will be.' 'You see that hotel,' replied Wigglesworth, pointing to his hotel. 'Be in front of that door in five minutes and I will pray for you and you will be as straight as any man in this place.' At that, he and his friend disappeared into the hotel, leaving the man stunned and staring after them,

After paying his hotel bill, Wigglesworth returned to the main door to find the man waiting nervously, looking, observed Wigglesworth, as if he was 'wondering if he was going to be trapped, or what was up that a man should stop in the street and tell him he should be made straight.

'It seemed difficult to get him from the elevator to my bedroom, as though Satan was making the last stroke for his life, but we got him there. Then in five minutes' time, this man walked out of that bedroom as straight as any man in this place. He walked perfectly and declared he hadn't a pain in his body.

'I had said it, so it must be,' said Wigglesworth, commenting on the incident. 'If you say anything you must stand with God to make it so. Never say anything for bravado, without you have the right to say it. Always be sure of your ground and that you are honouring God. If there is anything about it to make you anything, it will bring you sorrow.'

Moving on to Melbourne, Victoria, he preached at Good News Hall and a large circus arena called Wirth's Olympia, where it was estimated that approximately one thousand people accepted Christ as their Saviour during a series of meetings.

At one such meeting at the Olympia, Wigglesworth was pacing back and forth across the platform, unaware that he was moving ever closer to the front, until the inevitable happened. Swaying on the edge, his arms whirling like windmill sails in a desperate attempt to retain his balance, Wigglesworth toppled over, but surprisingly landed on his feet, the forward motion sending him staggering up the centre aisle, arms still flailing wildly. Reaching out to steady himself, he grasped the shoulder of a man sitting at the side of the aisle. At the end of the meeting, the man came to the platform to testify excitedly that the pain for which he was to request prayer, ceased as Wigglesworth placed his hand on his shoulder.

One of the most remarkable healings that took place in Melbourne was that of a woman suffering from a severe case of tuberculosis. The disease had attacked her internal organs, including her kidneys, which left her unable to eat without vomiting. Parts of her body were covered in running sores and the disease had eaten into the bone.

As the service progressed, her faith rose as she witnessed miracle after miracle. Finally, Wigglesworth came to her and as he prayed and anointed her with oil she felt the power of God go through her body. When she arrived home, she and her family removed the bandages covering the affected parts of her body and discovered that the ulcerated flesh had been replaced by new, healthy skin that was like that of a child.

Wigglesworth proceeded to Adelaide, where the salvations and miracles continued, although the meetings were not so well attended. One man came up for prayer with a badly poisoned hand and was due to go to hospital the following morning. 'Well, what's up with you?' probed Wigglesworth. When he was told, he replied, 'That's all right, the Lord knows all about that. Put your trust in the Lord and you'll be all right.' Then he moved on to the next person. A few minutes later he returned and asked the man to remove the bandages from his hand. When he did so, he discovered that the hand was completely healed. As a result of this miracle, the man and his wife and about forty others joined a recently established Pentecostal assembly, which provided impetus for the growth of the Pentecostal movement in South Australia.

Crossing the Tasman Sea, Smith Wigglesworth arrived in Wellington, the capital of New Zealand, at the end of May 1922. His host, Harry Roberts, had taken a step of faith and rented the largest auditorium in the city – the Town Hall – for the evening meetings, even though Wigglesworth was unknown in the country and little had been done to advertise his arrival.

The first night, approximately eight hundred people attended the service; the next night that had increased to sixteen hundred and by the third night the hall was filled to capacity with three thousand people. From then on, for the next three weeks of the campaign, hundreds were turned away each night, unable to gain admittance. Such was the demand for seats that an extraordinary phenomenon began to occur. As the start of that night's meeting drew near, people could be seen walking briskly through the streets of Wellington. When they neared the Town Hall, many would break into a run – indeed two young men were reported to have run two and a half miles, so determined were they to secure a precious seat.

One night, at least a thousand people were left waiting outside, unable to get in. Among them was a Salvation Army officer from Brisbane, Australia, who stood on the steps of the Town Hall and preached to the crowd. Around twenty accepted Christ and several remarkable healings occurred.

The *Dominion* newspaper sent a reporter to one of the meetings whose report under the headline 'Faith Healing – Extraordinary Scenes at Town Hall – The Deaf Made to Hear', proved to be a balanced, dispassionate account of the proceedings:

To heal the sick by Divine influence is no new claim, although to actually witness the process of cure being carried out in this workaday world has attracted big audiences to the Town Hall this week, a very large gathering being present at last night's demonstration.

The Yorkshire evangelist, Mr Smith-Wigglesworth, is conducting the proceedings, and, except that he anoints with oil, the real process of healing is carried out by faith itself. The evening commences with a religious service, including prayers and hymns, after which the demonstration of healing is given.

Last night about two hundred persons of both sexes presented themselves for treatment, but the evangelist was only able to deal with fifty of them, the other cases being postponed till tonight.

Those in search of relief comprised cripples (many of whom were able to throw away their crutches and sticks immediately); others, with goitre, rheumatism, partial blindness, deafness, and various forms of affliction. Quite a large percentage claimed that they were cured or relieved by the Divine faith poured into them by the evangelist.

To particularise: a woman of middle age, who was crippled with rheumatism, demonstrated her cure by walking across the floor; stutterers were almost instantly made to repeat the Lord's Prayer without stuttering; young women with necks swollen with goitre professed to be cured, and certainly the swellings in some cases disappeared or were reduced in size; an old man of 80 years, partially blind, said his sight had been improved; and numbers afflicted with pains of one sort and another declared that they were freed from their sufferings. There were failures, of course, due, perhaps, to lack of faith, or possibly the sufferers were incurable.[6]

The report proceeded to give more examples of miracles, concluding, 'And so it went on until fifty people had been treated and the healer was physically exhausted.'

Roberts also noted that hundreds who were unable to attend the meetings at the Town Hall were healed when they received handkerchiefs that Wigglesworth had prayed over. One was a girl with chronic hip disease who had been treated unsuccessfully for years. When she woke the next morning after placing the handkerchief on her hip, she discovered that she was completely healed.

Following the conclusion of his campaign in Wellington, Wigglesworth, accompanied by Roberts, crossed the Cook Strait to the South Island and held meetings in Christchurch, Dunedin and Blenheim. He then returned to Wellington at the beginning of July and held services at a Methodist church in the city.

As before, the church quickly filled to capacity and many had to be turned away. When Wigglesworth invited those who were sick to come forward for prayer, hundreds surged onto the platform, pinning him against the pulpit so that he was unable to move. Three policemen who were on duty at the meeting came to his rescue. The church vestry was opened and, with a policeman at each door, those seeking healing formed a line and entered one by one. Roberts reporting on the meetings said in awe, 'it seemed as though we were back in the days of Christ. The place was simply charged with an omnipotent Presence and we were all atremble.'[7]

Possibly the most memorable healing that night was that of an eleven-year-old boy suffering from infantile paralysis. His father carried the boy into the church, as his withered and twisted legs were too frail to support him. Wigglesworth told the father to put the child down and then cried, 'In the name of Jesus Christ, stand up!' As the power of the Holy Spirit surged through the boy's emaciated, useless legs they began to tremble and straighten out. The boy's father helped him to stand and then Wigglesworth, eyes blazing with intensity, commanded, 'Now walk, in the name of Jesus!' A crescendo of praise went up in the church as the boy, his spindly legs swinging back and forth, walked to one end of the vestry and back again. The father watched his son trembling, laughing and shouting with joy.

The meetings returned to the Town Hall, where a remarkable supernatural manifestation took place while Wigglesworth was relating to the audience the story of a young woman suffering from tuberculosis who was raised from the dead as he prayed. During the night, the woman had died and Satan appeared at the foot of the bed and sniggered malevolently at him, saying, 'I've got her safely held.' Recalled Wigglesworth, 'I seemed to be in hell and everything in the room turned to brass.'

Then, according to Roberts, an extraordinary phenomenon occurred:

That Wellington audience witnessed the most weird thing that ever happened in a public hall. Everything in the Town Hall appeared to turn to brass. What the Evangelist experienced in that death chamber was precipitated into the meeting by the power of the Spirit. That vast crowd just felt it had been ushered into the portals of hell itself. It was an ineffaceable and awful sensation. The lights, chairs, walls, the people, the grand organ all looked like solid brass. The tension [was] only broken when he [Wigglesworth] told how his own faith had fled away in the leering, faith-sapping presence of Satan himself. But he cried to God for help and pleaded the blood, and as he cried, the faith of God filled his soul.[8]

As Wigglesworth described how he saw the face of Jesus and the woman came back from the dead, the glinting brass was replaced by a warm glow that permeated the hall, breaking the unbearable tension and soliciting an audible sigh of relief. Such was the impact of that service, that around five hundred people gave their lives to Christ that night.

While Wigglesworth was in the midst of great revival in New Zealand, a letter arrived from America reminding him of his pledge to fulfil an engagement that had been arranged before he set out for the Antipodes. He replied, explaining that it was difficult for him to leave while a revival was taking place. Telegrams and letters passed between the two parties, but the church refused to relent and demanded that Wigglesworth come to America at the agreed date. Despite messages from thousands of New Zealanders pleading that Wigglesworth be allowed to stay, Wigglesworth was compelled to make the arduous three-week journey to the West Coast of America to con-duct a month-long series of meetings. In return, the church promised to pay his return voyage and give him a generous love offering. They also requested, and were granted, permission to print and sell his sermons.

Throughout the meetings, strident appeals were made for offerings for a new Bible school the church was build-ing. During his stay, the leaders of the church pleaded with him to release them from their promise to pay for his return fare. Wigglesworth explained to them that he needed the money to pay for his passage, pointing out that he had left revival and financial blessings in New Zealand because they had compelled him to come to America. Finally, under intense pressure he relented and absolved them from their obligations. The campaign was a great success, but Wigglesworth returned to New Zealand a wiser and poorer man.

After ministering in the United States, Wigglesworth crossed the border into Canada and conducted meetings in Montreal. It was there that he met a man who accompanied him to Vancouver, where they boarded a ship bound for New Zealand. The man, who was a race horse dealer, found himself strangely drawn to Wigglesworth, but spent the voyage discussing horse racing and playing cards.

When the ship docked for a few days in Fiji, Wigglesworth, as was his usual practice, preached and prayed for the sick on the islands. One day the race horse dealer staggered back to the ship deathly pale and shivering, his face a mask of fear and pain. Hammering desperately on Wigglesworth's door, he cried, 'I'm dying. I have been bitten by a snake!' His leg had turned a putrid dark green and had swollen up like a balloon. Wigglesworth opened the door and he staggered into the cabin, gasping, 'Can you help me?' Placing his hand on the snakebite, Wigglesworth shouted, 'In the name of Jesus, come out!' Before their eyes, the swelling went down and the man's leg returned to normal.

Wigglesworth arrived in Auckland, New Zealand in October 1923 where he held meetings until 3 December. He then travelled to the South Island to the town of Blenheim where his campaign commenced on 9 December in the Town Hall.

One of the reports of the meetings in the *Marlborough Express*, entitled 'Smith Wigglesworth Mission: A Wordy Evangelist', was dripping with scorn and sarcasm:

Disappointed in its claims to a visit by the more famous Hickson, Blenheim is apparently making the most of the next best thing in faith healers in the person of Mr Smith Wigglesworth, who opened a mission at the Town Hall yesterday, when he was welcomed by big congregations. Some months ago, a branch of the Wigglesworth mission was established in Blenheim by Mr Roberts, who conducted a faith healing session for a few days and apparently there are a goodly number of local adherents to the new fashion in religion.

Mr Roberts, by the way, is again to the fore in the present revival as Mr Smith Wigglesworth's right-hand man. Though the mission last night clashed with the regular church services, there was a big attendance, and it was noticeable that as the churches concluded their services, part of their congregations found their way to the Town Hall, so that the building was very well filled towards the end of the proceedings.

Mr Smith Wigglesworth is a big, brusque Yorkshireman who preaches a sermon like an endurance test. He commenced his discourse on the 'Four Square Gospel' before 7.30 last evening and he was still at it at 9 o'clock. Much of this sermon was tedious repetition and much of it arrant nonsense, but there was a certain oratory about the man which did something to relieve the tedium of his long discourse. Mr Smith Wigglesworth is not an educated man and he gloried in the fact that in all his life he had read no other book than the Bible. A little acquaintance with a few selected authors would enable him to better expound his doctrines and better interpret the 'Word of God', as he calls the Bible, but that does not seem to have occurred to him. Incidentally, he took the opportunity during the evening to refer to the case of a woman whose ear drums had been surgically removed, but who was able, immediately he laid hands on her, to hear a pin drop.

It may be remembered that when Mr Smith Wiggles-worth's disciple, Mr Roberts, was here some months ago, he also referred to this case and expressed some annoyance when the *Express* suggested that he was carried away by his enthusiasm. His statement is now confirmed by Mr Smith Wigglesworth, but that gentleman also claimed that he had seen dead people revived and brought back to life. The scep-tic can only conclude that the reports of these people's deaths had been much exaggerated and that the surgical removal of the lady's ear drums had been rather badly done. Faith, it is claimed, can move mountains, and there is hardly any question that so called 'faith healing' is effective in many neurotic cases, but even Mr Smith Wigglesworth's most ardent adherents can hardly expect to see new ear drums made to order while the patient waits, or new limbs sprout in place of amputated members, this being contrary to the common rules of Nature.

The report goes on to describe Wigglesworth's method of praying for people:

> With coat removed, he 'laid hands' very violently indeed on the afflicted parts of the various people's anatomy while he called in stentorian tones on the evil spirits possessing them to come out, and in one case dealt a frail lady such a smack in the stomach as might well have doubled her up. His patients, however, stood up unflinchingly to his assaults and in every case declared themselves improved in health by the encounter.[9]

Wigglesworth concluded his second evangelistic cam-paign in New Zealand in December 1924 and returned via the Pacific to conduct meetings in the United States at churches that included Bethel Temple in Los Angeles and the Maria Woodworth-Etter Tabernacle in Indianapolis.

In 1926, his international ministry continued with further visits to Switzerland (also in 1928 and 1929) and Ceylon, where he conducted a series of Easter meetings.

In 1927, Wigglesworth returned to Australia, this time accompanied by his daughter, Alice. Ministering at Richmond Temple in Melbourne, Wigglesworth prayed for the father of a Mr Harrison, who was suffering from cancer:

> My father was a Methodist preacher. He developed cancer of the throat and wore bandages around his throat at all times to hide and protect painful cancerous sores. He believed in a general way in prayer for healing, but hearing of Wigglesworth (and some of the claims made for his ministry), he decided to check him out.
>
> There was a meeting at Richmond Temple, Melbourne and he went to see for himself. As he listened, he was convinced and went forward for prayer at the end of the service. Smith Wigglesworth asked him what was wrong, then slapped my father's neck hard. The astonishing thing was that my father could hardly stand even the bandages around his throat because his neck was so painful, but when Wigglesworth slapped him, he felt no pain at all. In fact, he didn't even notice the slap!
>
> Then Wigglesworth said to him, 'Go home. Take those bandages off in the morning and you will find the growths have gone.' He returned home, went to bed and slept when previously severe pain had kept him awake for hours. The next morning, my father removed the bandages and the growths had disappeared entirely. There was not even a scar or mark left.[10]

Another case in the town of Naremburn in New South Wales in 1927 was that of a woman who had suffered a serious accident which had severely damaged her knee.

Synovitis and chronic arthritis had set in. Her suffering was compounded when she ruptured muscle fibres in her other leg:

On one leg I had a steel and leather apparatus to keep the knee joint from locking and pinching, which caused intense pain, and the other was in tight bandages. With the aid of a pair of crutches, I got out to the car to be taken to the meeting and though suffering intensely, I believed I would be healed. After the address I joined with those who were to be ministered to, and as the evangelist [Wigglesworth] laid his hands on me and prayed I had a strange yet beautiful experience as though cold water with great force was being sprayed in jets upon both of my afflicted members where they were injured. So strong seemed to be the force that it even hurt me, and I knew it was the Lord, but on turning away I didn't feel any better and expressed my disappointment to two or three.

All the way home I wept copiously and poured out my heart to God and continued to say, 'Lord, I believe, help Thou my unbelief.' Arriving home, I was helped out of the car and after walking a few steps said that I thought I could walk alone. Just as I reached the threshold of the door, a wall of bright shining light confronted me, so exceedingly bright that it almost staggered me and instantly I cried out, 'Glory to God, I'm healed!' and truly I was. I went through the house praising the Lord and up and down the back verandah, glorifying God and walking as I did before meeting with the accident. Seeing the crutches, I said, 'Take those back to the kind friend that loaned them to me. I shall not want them any more.' So the crutches were returned just before midnight. Hallelujah![11]

The same year, he left Australia, accompanied by Alice, and sailed to Vancouver, before arriving in Los Angeles where he preached at Aimee Semple Macpherson's (1890–1944) church, Angelus Temple in Los Angeles, a cavernous edifice built in 1923 that could seat five thousand people. According to Wigglesworth, he had greater anointing there to minister than at any place he had ever been and he preached at the church on a number of occasions.

In May of 1929, eight years after his first crusade in Scandinavia, he responded to requests to return to Norway and Sweden. In Norway, in the small fishing town of Haügesund on the west coast, the hall hosting Wigglesworth's meetings was so full that he and his interpreter were unable to get in the door. The only solution was to hoist them through a window straight onto the platform. When Wigglesworth left for the town of Stavanger, a great throng of people came to the quayside to see him off. As he waited for the ship to cast off its moorings, Wigglesworth began preaching and then sang his signature refrain, 'Only believe, only believe, all things are possible, only believe', his booming Yorkshire voice echoing through the fjord.

The decade came to a close with a further visit to Switzerland, followed by meetings in the United States in September.

During the 1920s, Wigglesworth also ministered at Pentecostal assemblies in Holland, Belgium and Italy and ventured to Palestine and Egypt, where he spent a month preaching and teaching. In Jerusalem, he described holding services for weeks on the Mount of Olives and outside the Damascus Gate, where many were filled with the Holy Spirit, and at a prison in the city. Staying at a guest house at the foot of Mount Carmel, he expressed his delight in being able to wake up in the morning and look across the Sea of Galilee to the place described in the Gospels where Christ cast out a legion of demons and allowed them to enter a herd of pigs that subsequently stampeded to their death into the lake.

Once when Wigglesworth was visiting the Wailing Wall in Jerusalem he observed some young men weeping bitterly and crying, 'Lord, how long, Lord, how long?' Filled with compassion and burning with zeal he preached the gospel to them. The next day, ten of the men came to see him with a rabbi, saying, 'Where did the fire come from?'

He had such an impact in Jerusalem that his train to Alexandria in Egypt via the port of Haifa was delayed so that he could finish his sermon to the people who had thronged the railway station to see him off. For half an hour, Wigglesworth preached about Christ, with tears running down his face, and he was to recall with amusement that he was probably the first Gentile preacher to receive an offering from the Jews in the Holy Land.

As he boarded the train to Alexandria, where he was to take a ship to Venice in Italy, he was approached by some Jewish men, including a rabbi, who expressed their desire to travel with him on the train. Throughout the journey Wigglesworth expounded the Scriptures, proving that Christ is the Messiah as the men listened, captivated. When they arrived at the city, they insisted on taking him to dinner to continue their discussion. One said to Wigglesworth, 'There is something about your preaching that is different from the rabbi.'

'Well, what is it?' enquired Wigglesworth.

'Oh, you moved us! There was a warmth about it!' he replied, eyes lighting up as the others nodded animatedly.

Gazing at the men, Wigglesworth said, 'Yes, Brother. It isn't law. The glory position is that it is warm. You feel it. It is regenerative. It is quickening. It moves your human nature. It makes you know that this is life divine.'

They listened attentively as he continued with his simple gospel message and then remarked, 'Oh, but it is so different!'

'Yes,' Wigglesworth repeated, 'and the day is coming when your veil will be taken from your eyes and you will see this Messiah.'

Following dinner, they had to leave, but they did so reluctantly, wanting to talk more. No more is heard about these men, but one can imagine that they were never the same after their encounter with Smith Wigglesworth.

In Alexandria, Wigglesworth boarded a ship bound for Venice. While on board, he was as eager as ever to preach the gospel, but was frustrated by the lack of an interpreter. Undaunted, he prayed that God would somehow provide an opportunity for him to witness and then, where he stood on deck, a man suddenly spun round three times and collapsed. His wife cried out panic-stricken, 'My husband is dead!' As a passenger ran for the ship's doctor, Wigglesworth stood over the body and commanded the spirit of death to leave in the name of Jesus. The man came back to life, to the amazement and joy of his wife, and from then on, the ship was alive with excitement as news spread like wildfire that a man had been raised from the dead. Wigglesworth was able to find five people who could interpret for him and never looked back. 'I preached the gospel in the power of the Holy Ghost and it was wonderful, the people crying for mercy on every side.'

Chapter Eleven

TRIUMPHING OVER TRIALS

One day in 1930, Smith Wigglesworth was seized by an acute pain in his side. The pain, instead of abating became more severe and Wigglesworth, doubled up in agony, collapsed on the bedroom floor, crying out for his son-in-law, James Salter. Later, he was shocked to discover the cause of his distress when he passed a number of jagged kidney stones, the first of many over the coming months. It was the beginning of the greatest physical trial of his life and one that he would endure for three long years.

For the first time in his years of ministry, Wigglesworth was forced to decline invitations to preach, but when an urgent request arrived during the winter of 1930–31 to pray for some sick people on the Isle of Man, his compassionate heart compelled him to go. This entailed a three-hour trip by rail, before a rough sea passage to the island. When he arrived he was met by a relative, a nurse, who, when she saw how ill and haggard he looked, pleaded with him to go straight to bed, but he insisted on praying for those who needed healing. On the return journey, he struggled to pass stones and haemorrhaged so much blood that – deathly pale and shivering – his companions wrapped him in rugs in an attempt to keep him warm.

In the midst of his ill health, Wigglesworth left, in May 1931, for evangelistic campaigns in Sweden, Norway, Denmark and Finland. Night after night, he would be in and out of bed as he battled to expel the stones, often rolling on the floor in agony, only to rise twice daily to minister.

According to James Salter, when Wigglesworth was preaching in the United States in the spring of 1932, he was in constant discomfort and was bleeding profusely. He stayed in bed during the day, went by taxi to the meetings in the evening and then came immediately back to his hotel. At times during the meetings, when he could endure the pain no longer, he would dash off the platform, seek a place where he could pass some more stones and then return to the meeting to continue the service. This went on day after day, but Wigglesworth preached with great power and anointing and there were many miracles, even though he was more ill than many of the people who came forward seeking his prayers for healing.

This was something that perplexed Wigglesworth, for no doubt he laid hands on himself and prayed for his own healing. In one service he said, 'I do not understand the ways of God. Here He is healing under my ministry and yet as I am preaching to you, I am suffering excruciating pains from kidney stones coming down from my body.' It was also in a service during this campaign that Wigglesworth announced that he had asked God for fifteen more years in which to serve Him. As it transpired, his request was granted down to the very week.

James Salter, who, with Alice, witnessed many of Wigglesworth's struggles said later:

Living with him, sharing his bedroom as we frequently did during those years, we marvelled at the unquenched zeal in

his fiery preaching and his compassionate ministry to the
sick. I do not remember his ever absenting himself from any
meeting during the period, although there were times when
he had to leave the preaching to others. Knowing him as
perhaps no other man did, being together under the most
intimate conditions, sharing mutual secrets, having every
opportunity to weigh and assess him physically and spiritually, one cannot find the answer to the struggle of those days
and years in the iron constitution and will of steel, both of
which he possessed; for I have seen things break down under
lesser tests. He did not just bear those agonies; he made them
serve the purpose of God and gloried in and over them.[1]

After two years of unrelenting torment, Wigglesworth was
persuaded to consult a physician who, after an examination, advised him to have an X-ray. This revealed the presence of a large, bean-shaped kidney stone in his bladder.

The doctor, shocked at how advanced the condition
was, advised Wigglesworth to have an immediate operation to remove the stone to save him from prolonged suffering and possible death. With the doctor poised to call
the hospital to arrange a bed, Wigglesworth gazed at his
anxious face and remarked calmly, 'Doctor, the God who
made this body is the one who can cure it. No knife shall
ever cut it so long as I live.'

Staggered by Wigglesworth's unexpected reply, the
doctor stammered, 'What about these stones?'

'God will deal with them,' retorted Wigglesworth with
an air of finality.

'Well, if He ever does, I shall be interested to know
about it,' replied the doctor sarcastically.

'You shall,' said Wigglesworth, and promptly left the
surgery.

A vessel was provided at home specially for his use
and once when Alice went to empty it she discovered a

thick, grey sediment at the bottom containing a gritty substance resembling broken nutshells. When Wigglesworth was shown what he had passed he remarked: 'This is the beginning of the end. The Lord has operated.' Relief would indeed come, but he had to endure many more months of excruciating pain as he strained to pass one stone after another.

Then, on 4 October 1933, at around four o'clock in the afternoon, the miracle commenced. For hours, Wigglesworth grimaced in agony as he excreted grit and sharp granite-like stones, some three eighths of an inch long, nine of which he kept in a bottle to show people. As he promised, he returned to see the doctor who had advised him to have an operation and showed him the last stone that he had passed. The doctor examined it and admitted that it was a miracle that he had been able to expel such an object. Those who knew Wigglesworth believed that he mellowed following this experience and became more compassionate.

Following his healing, Wigglesworth ministered extensively in Europe, returning to Norway, Sweden and Switzerland and to the United States. One service, held at the Old Fashioned Tabernacle in Washington DC in March 1935, the subject of which was 'Fear not; only believe', was recorded in detail by James H. Taylor:

His first appeal was to those who desired salvation and about twenty people responded. After this he asked those who were seeking healing to assemble in the space between the platform and the wall on the left of the hall. One hundred people responded. Turning to them he said, 'Look at me and listen. I want this thought [to] take possession of you: "I'm going to be healed." Second: be sure to understand that I never healed anyone, and I never saw anyone heal another, but I have seen the power of God work through men and heal. Hallelujah.'

He came down from the platform and reaching the head of the long line, he began to lay hands upon them, commanding diseases and demons in the name of Jesus to depart from them. They shook when he touched them, some jumped, some shouted, some were prostrated and many testified to healing.

I think it will help our testimony to state that we had seats in the second row (front) from the healing corner, so that what happened during the healing hour was almost within hand reach.

Just before the meeting began, we had noticed that a young girl with crutches was coming in, assisted by a man and a woman. Her legs absolutely dangled, with the feet hanging vertically from them. From her waist she seemed limp and powerless. Room was made for her in the front row. When the invitation to be saved was given, she attempted to go forward aided by her assistants. Brother Wigglesworth, on seeing her start said, 'You stay right where you are. You are going to be a different girl when you leave this place.' When the rest had been dealt with, Brother Wigglesworth turned to the girl and, having been told her trouble, said to the people, 'This girl has no muscles in her legs; she never walked before.' He laid his hands on her head and prayed and cried, 'In the name of Jesus Christ, walk!' Looking at her, he said, 'You are afraid aren't you?' 'Yes,' she replied. 'There is no need to be. You are healed!' He shouted, 'Walk, Walk!' And praise God she did – like a baby just learning. Twice she walked, in that characteristic way, the length of the platform. Glory to God. When we left the room her crutches were lying on the seat. On reaching the sidewalk we saw her standing, as others do, talking with two girl friends.

The woman who assisted her forward was her mother, and the man was her uncle, who wept like a child during her healing, who testified in the evening meeting that she walked up the stairs at her home without assistance, repeated the fact that she had never walked before, stating also that her mother, who went forward for healing for a bunch in her breast, when asked about it said, 'It's gone!'

Wonderful things happened in the evening meeting also. Our brother testified to healing of cancer of two years' standing. A poor sick man whom the doctors had given up, whose legs were useless, except for slow motion, was healed and ran twice around the hall. When asked how many had been healed during the week's services, at least two hundred rose.

Sadly, when Taylor eagerly scanned many of the newspapers the following day, he did not find a single report of the meeting.

Also in 1935, Wigglesworth stopped for one day in Springfield, Missouri, which was the last time that Stanley Frodsham saw him. There were many healings that day, including a serious case of cancer. A man was brought to the morning service whose face was contorted with pain. Wigglesworth said to him, 'Man, will you believe the Lord if He heals you?' When the man was too incoherent to answer, Wigglesworth clapped his hand on the cancer on the man's forehead and in the name of Jesus cursed it. His whole countenance changed when he realised the pain had gone. However, three days later, a phone call came from the man as the pain had returned. For days to come further requests came for prayer as he endured agonising pain. After two weeks, he decided to consult some doctors and after an examination they told him, 'You are mighty lucky. That cancer is withered up at the roots and will soon be ready to drop out.' A few days later, it was gone and only a faint scar was left on his forehead where the tumour had been.

In the summer of 1936, Smith Wigglesworth sailed for South Africa with Alice for what was to prove his last and most prominent crusade of the decade. Yet it was also the one he considered his most arduous. When it came time for him to leave he was suffering intensely from sciatica, locking his legs and causing him to have to hobble grimacing up the gangplank and endure the gnawing pain throughout most of the long voyage.

When Wigglesworth arrived in Cape Town in October, there were astonishing scenes of jubilation as the seventy-seven-year-old evangelist was mobbed by ecstatic crowds wherever he went. One man even came up to him and hugged and kissed him.

During the first meeting at the town hall, Wigglesworth noticed a man stricken with cancer and said to the audience, 'There is a man in this place suffering tremendously. He does not even know I am talking about him. I give you the choice. If you want me to deliver that man so that he can enjoy the meeting, I will go down in the name of the Lord and deliver him, or I will preach . . . I went down and the people saw what God can do. They saw that man shouting and raving, for he was like an intoxicated man. He was shouting, "I was bound but now I am free!" It was a wonderful thing to see that man changed.'

In the town of Harrismith, a woman who was unable to walk and who had spent hundreds of pounds on operations was instantly healed as Wigglesworth laid hands on her. 'As if a cannon had blown her up, she rose and I thought her husband would go mad with joy and excitement because he saw his wife mightily moved by the power of God, made free, the first in the meetings afterwards to glorify God.'

Driven by a young assistant pastor called Basil Crompton, who had read *Ever Increasing Faith* and as a consequence received salvation and healing of tuberculosis, Wigglesworth travelled thousands of miles across South Africa in a vehicle purchased by Crompton specially for the trip, including the veld where he ministered to the Zulu tribes.

One night, Wigglesworth and the Salters returned to their hotel after a particularly strenuous service when many received prayer. James Salter, who had arrived from the Belgian Congo to travel with Wigglesworth and Alice for two weeks, was helping him get ready for bed when Wigglesworth suddenly locked the door and revealed that he had been ruptured badly. He believed that it was due to getting in and out of cars, which may have exacerbated the problem, but it was more likely that it occurred when he leapt off a platform while ministering at a service. As Wigglesworth continued to minister powerfully, only Alice and James Salter knew how much pain and discomfort he was enduring.

'How he worked and preached!' marvelled Salter. 'There were meetings in large halls and he travelled thousands of miles over corrugated dirt roads, preaching and praying for the sick, both black and white, eating unusual food, perspiring in the hot sun, and yet he never spared himself. He certainly did not behave like a badly ruptured man. It was another of the secrets that God and he shared and overcame.'

On 4 November 1936, Wigglesworth ministered in Wynberg, Cape Province at the 650-seat Town Hall, which that night was crammed with around a thousand people. A minister, Ralph Coates, reporting on the meeting, was to say that he had never observed such remarkable scenes of revival and miracles:

There was no standing room and the people crowded on the platform. All shades and conditions were represented. Mohammedans, Malays, Jews, Coloured, maimed, impotent, crippled, paralysed and cancerous pressed in for promised help. Mrs Salter and Mr Wigglesworth preached Jesus

Christ as the living Word and under the unction of the Holy
Ghost.

On 5th and 6th and two meetings on 8th, I should esti-
mate that 600 stood to receive salvation through the blood of
Jesus. After these conversions in each meeting, pains immediately disappeared in answer to prayer from the platform.
On 6th and 8th the crowd of the 5th had increased, until
those outside were as many as those inside the hall. Never
had Wynberg had such a visitation and never had the need
of the healing touch of Jesus been so manifest, and God met
us and the need.

I have in my study the crutches of one coloured girl, crippled, but healed instantly. One elderly man, whom I assisted
into the hall, so bound with rheumatism that he could not sit,
flourished his crutches in the air as God immediately met
him in prayer and he walked triumphantly out of the hall. In
four cases of terrible cancer the pain ceased immediately
hands were laid on the sufferers. The halt walked normally,
deaf ears were unstopped and the blind saw.

During his South African campaign, Wigglesworth
became friends with David du Plessis (1905–1987), then
the thirty-one-year-old general secretary of the Apostolic
Faith Mission in South Africa, but later to become one of
the most prominent evangelists of the twentieth century
and known universally as Mr Pentecost.

One morning in 1936, du Plessis arrived at his office in
Johannesburg early to clear his desk so that he could
devote the rest of the day to his house guest – Smith
Wigglesworth – whom he had travelled with and for
whom he had acted, on occasion, as interpreter.

As he was to relate in his autobiography, *A Man Called
Mr Pentecost*, du Plessis was hunched over his desk fully
absorbed in writing a letter when, without warning, the
door suddenly swung open. He looked up startled by the

sudden noise to see Wigglesworth standing in the doorway. Smiling in relief and recognition, he began to speak and then stopped, his smile vanishing as he glimpsed Wigglesworth's stern expression.

'Come out here!' thundered Wigglesworth. Without hesitating, du Plessis obeyed. As soon as he had stepped outside the door, Wigglesworth placed his hands firmly on his shoulders and pressed him against the wall. Gazing at du Plessis, his eyes boring into his with an almost unbearable intensity he declared:

I have been sent by the Lord to tell you what he has shown me this morning. Through the old-line denominations will come revival that will eclipse anything we have known through history. No such things have happened in times past as will happen when this begins.

It will eclipse the present-day twentieth-century Pentecostal revival that already is a marvel to the world with its strong opposition from the established church. But this same blessing will become acceptable to the churches and they will go on with this message and this experience beyond what the Pentecostals have achieved. You will live to see this work grow to such dimensions that the Pentecostal movement itself will be a light thing in comparison with what God will do through the old churches.[2] There will be tremendous gatherings of people, unlike anything we've seen, and great leaders will change their attitude and accept not only the message but also the blessing.[3]

Recalling the incident some years later, du Plessis said, 'Wigglesworth paused at this point, ever so lightly, as his eyes burned into mine.' Then he added, 'The Lord said to me that I am to give you warning that he is going to use you in this movement. You will have a prominent part.' He paused briefly, his eyes never leaving du Plessis' and then concluded his message to the stunned South African. 'One final word, the last word the Lord gave me for you. All he requires of you is that you be humble and faithful. You will live to see the whole fulfilled.'

Then bowing his head, Wigglesworth said quietly, 'Lord, I have delivered the message of what you are planning to do with this young man. And now, Lord, bless him and get him ready. Keep him in good health so that all this may come to pass. Amen.' Wigglesworth released his grip on du Plessis, turned and left without another word, closing the door quietly behind him.

Leaning, stunned, against the wall for a few minutes, it occurred to du Plessis to run after Wigglesworth to question him about the remarkable message he had delivered, but he decided against it, instead returning to his chair in a daze, his mind trying to recall all that had been said.

About ten minutes later, as he was still mulling over the extraordinary experience that had just transpired, there was a faint knock at the door. Wondering whom it could be, he got up and opened the door. To his astonishment, it was Wigglesworth, who, smiling and with an outstretched hand, greeted du Plessis warmly, saying, 'Good morning, Brother David. How are you this morning?'

A frowning du Plessis grasped his hand limply: 'About now, very puzzled,' he replied.

'And why is that?' enquired Wigglesworth in apparent innocence.

'Well now,' said du Plessis, 'you come into this office and you stand me against the wall and you prophesy and now you come back in acting as if you'd never seen me before. And you want to know why I'm puzzled?'

Unruffled, Wigglesworth explained to a dumbfounded du Plessis that in Old Testament times, when God gave a message to the prophets he warned them to 'speak to no man on the way'. Taking the Scriptures literally as always, that is exactly what he did, even ignoring the young minister's wife that morning.

Wigglesworth then went on to explain that he awoke at du Plessis' home well before dawn that morning and had been given this message from God in the form of a series of visions. 'I even argued with the Lord about it,' smiled Wigglesworth. 'This is not what my brethren expect.' Du Plessis could only nod in agreement, for he had been convinced that the Lord had passed over the established denominations and that they were virtually apostate.

'At times,' continued Wigglesworth, 'I didn't know whether I was asleep or not, it was so much like a dream. I was completely relaxed and felt good, and then I realised the Lord was speaking to me. Finally, He said, "You must tell this to David, give him warning; he is to have a prominent part in this."'

Du Plessis sat in awed silence, trying to come to terms with the sheer enormity of the prophecy, until Wigglesworth enquired, 'You got it?'

'Yes, I've got it,' replied du Plessis. 'I think I will never forget it. But you have to understand. I just can't accept everything you've said. If it's going to happen and I'm supposed to be involved in it, the Lord will have to speak to me himself.'

'That's wisdom,' Wigglesworth shot back quickly. 'Don't act just on what I or anybody else says. The Lord will tell you. But for now He wants you to have this warning – because it's coming, that's for sure. He will prepare you in the Spirit. But remember, it won't come tomorrow. It will not even begin during my lifetime. The day I pass away, then you can begin to think about it.'

Moving a step closer to du Plessis, Wigglesworth probed, 'Do you ever get airsick?' Perplexed, du Plessis answered that he had never even flown in a plane. 'Do you ever get seasick?' enquired Wigglesworth again. Wondering where this line of questioning was leading, du Plessis replied that he had never been to sea either.

'Well,' said Wigglesworth, 'you are going to travel more that most men. I saw it in the vision.'

Drawing closer still to du Plessis, Wigglesworth commanded, 'Come out of there.' With a little trepidation, du Plessis came out from behind his desk and Wigglesworth again laid his hand on the young minister's shoulder and prayed, 'Lord, you've shown me what you have for this young man in his future and now I pray that he will never take ill when he travels in your service.'

Three weeks after this incident, du Plessis received a letter from the Assemblies of God inviting him to speak at the denomination's general council in 1937, a considerable honour for an unknown South African. Examining the date when the letter was posted, du Plessis realised that it had been sent before Wigglesworth had prophesied to him. Before replying to the letter, du Plessis decided to seek Wigglesworth's counsel, and travelled to Cape Town where he was holding a crusade. When he was informed of the invitation, Wigglesworth couldn't resist a smile. 'I told you the Lord is going to prepare you for this great move. This is just one of the steps.'

Not long before Wigglesworth's death, du Plessis had what was to prove his final encounter with the evangelist, who said to him softly, 'My brother David, I've had no further word from the Lord. But I am absolutely sure that what He revealed in South Africa is coming and that you are the man for it.'

Wigglesworth's prophecy would indeed, in time, be fulfilled, but not before du Plessis would be first elevated and then rejected by members of the Pentecostal Church, suffer financial hardship and be involved in a major car accident. This incident not withstanding, he would travel more than a million miles over land, sea and air preaching the gospel in fifty-six countries without becoming ill.

Through the 1950s and 60s, du Plessis, overcoming his deep-seated prejudice against the established denominations, forged links with the World Council of Churches and was invited to the world conference of the organisation's missionary arm in 1952. It was an event so genuinely ecumenical that du Plessis remarked that it was 'enough to bring a smile to Wigglesworth's face'.

To his surprise, he found a hunger for knowledge about the Pentecostal experience even among the Roman Catholic Church hierarchy with whom he held discussions at the Vatican Council in 1964. The interest in Pentecost grew within the Catholic Church and led to the holding of the Congress on the Charismatic Renewal in the Catholic Church in 1975 at St Peter's Basilica in Rome. One of the highlights was a Mass on Pentecost Sunday attended by twenty thousand believers and presided over by Pope Paul VI, at which there were speaking and singing in tongues and prophetic utterances.

The following day, nearly twelve thousand delegates from sixty nations, including seven hundred priests and twelve bishops, gathered at the Basilica to celebrate the closing Eucharist. That night, as he lay in bed, du Plessis marvelled at how the Roman Catholic Church had accepted and embraced Pentecost. 'I closed my eyes and was on the brink of sleep,' recalled du Plessis. 'In my mind's eye, I could see, as plain as life, standing erect and stern before me, a mighty man of God – Smith Wigglesworth. Slowly his sternness gave way to a contented grin.'

Du Plessis' involvement with the Catholic Church culminated in an audience with the Pope at the Vatican during the fifth session of the Pentecostal–Roman Catholic dialogue. This had commenced in 1971 and comprised three Pentecostals, three main-line Protestants and three Catholics. As Pope Paul was introduced to the Pentecostal group, he came to du Plessis, whose name was announced. The Pope gazed at him and said, 'So you are Mr Pentecost?' 'That's what they call me,' du Plessis replied. The year was 1976: forty years after Smith Wigglesworth had pinned du Plessis to the wall of the young minister's office in Johannesburg and delivered his prophetic message.

According to George Stormont, Wigglesworth prophesied again during a crusade a week before his death. His prophecy described a two-fold move of the Holy Spirit: the first would bring the restoration of the gifts of the Spirit; the second would bring a revival of emphasis on the Bible. 'When these two moves of the Spirit combine,' declared Wigglesworth, 'we shall see the greatest move the Church of Jesus Christ has ever seen.'

Chapter Twelve

AND THEN HE WAS NOT;
FOR GOD TOOK HIM

The outbreak of the Second World War, in September
1939, brought an end to Smith Wigglesworth's evangelistic campaigns abroad (although his last was, in effect, in
South Africa in 1936–7), but not his ministry in the British
Isles. Now in his eighties, Wigglesworth preached at
meetings throughout the country and continued to chair
the annual Easter Preston Convention. In October 1941,
for instance, it was reported that Wigglesworth 'is still
active and has ministered recently in the Full Gospel
Church at Leamington Spa, where twelve were filled with
the Holy Spirit.' Then, in the following year, according to
another account, he travelled on a packed train from his
home in Bradford to Boston in Lincolnshire where he
preached powerfully and prayed for the sick.

Now that Wigglesworth was travelling less, he was
able to visit his friends more often, including George
Stormont, who recalled the times when Wigglesworth
would stay with him at his home in Leigh-on-Sea, Essex
during the 1940s. Day after day, Wigglesworth would sit,
immaculately dressed, on a bench in gardens above the
railway station, praying and meditating on the Word to

see 'what Father had to say'. From his vantage point, he could observe people trudging up the 150 steps from the station. Some who were elderly would stagger to the top, cheeks crimson and wheezing heavily. As they fought for breath, Wigglesworth, with a heart consumed with concern and compassion, would call out with astonishing frankness, 'Are you ready to die?' Stunned at first by the baldness of the statement, but then recognising his sincerity, few took offence and several accepted Christ following his ministry to them.

On another occasion, he watched a young couple sullenly climb the steps, a telling distance between them. When they reached the top, he enquired in a kindly voice whether they had quarrelled. It transpired that they had. And as they declared bitterly that their marriage was over, Wigglesworth beckoned them to sit either side of him and, with a fatherly arm around each, he listened with compassion as they poured out their hearts. By the time he had finished ministering to them, they went on their way arm in arm with their eyes liquid with tears, both their souls and their marriage saved.

Once during the war years, Wigglesworth's friend and assistant pastor of Bridge Street Church in Leeds, George Miles, visited him at his home in Bradford with an American minister who had preached at his church. Five times during their visit, Wigglesworth interrupted the conversation and opened his New Testament to 'hear what the Father had to say'. He then read some verses, followed by a brief exhortation and prayer. 'I was profoundly aware that God was in that place,' recalled Miles. 'Even during dinner, we heard again, "what the Father had to say".'

At the conclusion of the meal, Wigglesworth asked Miles whether he had any petrol in his car, a valid question, as fuel was strictly rationed at the time and was supposed to be used only for essential travel. When Miles replied that he had, Wigglesworth informed him that they would go for a short trip. Miles had a few reservations about using the precious fuel for what appeared to be nothing more than a visit to the countryside, but it was difficult to argue with a man like Wigglesworth.

Wigglesworth asked the American visitor to sit in the rear, while he sat in the front passenger seat to guide Miles. As soon as he sat down, he lifted up his hands and prayed, 'Lord, bless this young man. Bless this car,' and then he added, 'Lord, bless these tyres.' Miles was to say later that he said a fervent 'Amen' to this prayer because one of the tyres on the car, which were synthetic due to war-time shortages of rubber, had, unknown to Wigglesworth, a gaping whole through which the inner tube was visible.

They travelled some distance before arriving at the edge of Ilkley Moor. Leading up to the moor was an unpaved track, strewn with jagged stones. To Miles' astonishment and trepidation, Wigglesworth waved him on saying, 'Ah, yes. This is the road we want. Go straight ahead, young man.' Miles nervously inched the car forward onto the narrow road and drove, expecting to hear a loud bang as the inner tube was punctured, but they arrived at the moor without incident.

They sat on a bench for a while and listened, captivated, as Wigglesworth recounted some of his experiences on the mission field. Then Miles and the American minister decided to go for a stroll, leaving Wigglesworth to sit in the sun in solitude for a few moments.

When they returned, they found Wigglesworth kneeling with a man at the bench, both immersed in fervent prayer. As they continued praying, Miles sensed the same holy atmosphere that he had experienced at Wigglesworth's home. As the two men rose from their knees,

Wigglesworth said to Miles, 'Now, young man, this brother has to go in to the hospital tomorrow for a major operation. He used to be a servant of God, but had back-slidden and got right away from the Saviour. But today, he has come back home to God and now, whatever happens in the hospital, his soul is right with God.'

After the man, his face radiant, explained excitedly how his faith had been restored, Wigglesworth said, 'I knew I had to come here today. Father sent me. Now our task is fulfilled, we will give glory to God as we return home.' They drove back down the unpaved road and arrived back in Leeds with the inner tube still poking through the worn tyre.

When he was at home in Bradford, Wigglesworth would often stroll down to nearby Manningham Park, sit on a bench and bask in the sun. These periods of relaxation were, as always, times of potential ministry. One man who accompanied him to the park one afternoon testified that while there he led two people to Christ and prayed for the healing of two others. 'He seemed so busy that my friend and I decided to take a short walk. When we returned we found him kneeling by the side of another man pointing him to the Lord Jesus.' At other times, recalled his friend, Albert Hibbert, Wigglesworth would say nothing at all. But such was his anointing that he would always impart something to those who sat beside him.

It was also in Manningham Park, one hot autumn day in 1944, that Wigglesworth suffered a severe bout of sunstroke. When he staggered home at midday, Alice and James Salter noticed immediately that he was partially paralysed on one side and that his speech was slurred. When a doctor was called out to examine him, an incoherent Wigglesworth pleaded with him to be left alone. The doctor, who had once advised him to have an operation only to be bluntly rebuffed, thought it was resentment, but Wigglesworth was too ill to recognise him. Later the doctor confided to Salter that his father-in-law could die at any moment. Despite the gloomy prognosis, after two days rest, Wigglesworth was able to rise from his bed and the first thing that he did was apologise to the doctor, explaining to him that he was unaware of what he was saying or doing. However, he was weakened by the stroke, both mentally and physically and, unsteady on his legs, suffered a number of bad falls.

Throughout that winter, the Salters cared for the ageing patriarch, preparing his meals and ensuring he was wrapped up against the cold. Then, in the spring of 1945, Wigglesworth experienced a miraculous healing and appeared to have made a full recovery. He began writing all his own letters again and by the time of the Easter convention, of which he was chairman as usual, he was bursting to testify about how God had restored his health. A report of the convention that year declared that:

> Brother Wigglesworth had a marvellous testimony of renewed life and caught his spirit of earlier days. He told how that last year it was feared that he was passing away but God quickened the mortal body of his servant. It was apparent to all that our esteemed brother, who is 86 years old, had a supernatural experience. Notwithstanding the fact that there were three meetings each day during the four days, Brother Wigglesworth never missed a meeting, lifting the great congregation into heights of expectation by his words of faith. This living exhibition of God's quickening power stimulated the faith of all, especially those who were seeking God for divine healing.

Often throughout the Easter convention he was heard to utter, 'Why, I don't know that I have a body!' But age was catching up with even the indefatigable Wigglesworth.

James and Alice Salter noticed how haggard and drawn he looked when they collected him from Bradford railway station after he returned from a convention where his ministry was intensive, even by his standards. That evening, during their usual time of prayer, Wigglesworth remarked sadly, 'I cannot understand some of these young preachers these days. Fancy a man of my age preaching three times a day and praying for the sick at each service. Some of them will take the afternoon off and go to bed, leaving me to preach. When I was their age, I would preach all the day and then pray and tarry all night with those who were seeking to be filled with the Holy Spirit.'

The last time that Albert Hibbert had fellowship with Wigglesworth was at his home a week before he died. Gazing at Hibbert, Wigglesworth's eyes filled with tears. 'When are you going to move into the realm that you have not yet touched and get going for God?' challenged Wigglesworth. 'I am an old man, eighty-seven years of age. I may not look it; I certainly don't feel it. But you cannot argue with the birth certificate and it tells me I am eighty-seven. So I have to accept it, regardless of how I feel about it.

'Today in my mail I had an invitation to Australia, one to India and Ceylon, and one to America. People have their eyes on me.' Then, sobbing, he said, 'Poor Wigglesworth. What a failure to think that people have their eyes on me. God will never give His glory to another; He will take me from the scene.'

The winter of 1946–7 was the most severe for two hundred years and the whole of Britain shivered in sub-zero temperatures. At Victor Road, Bradford, Smith Wigglesworth, now in his eighty-eighth year, had spent much of the winter months indoors, avoiding the bad weather. But when, in March 1947, he was informed of the death of his dear friend Wilfred Richardson, he was determined to attend the funeral at Glad Tidings Hall in Wakefield, against the advice of the Salters and his doctor. 'I must attend his funeral,' he thundered to his concerned daughter and son-in-law, who realised that it was futile to try to persuade him otherwise.

About ten weeks earlier, Wigglesworth had visited Richardson in hospital, where he was recovering from a major operation. 'What will they say,' wailed Richardson in anguish, his eyes welling up with tears. 'What can I tell my people? I who have preached divine healing for over thirty years and now in the hospital and have submitted to an operation!' Despite the counsel of his friend and fellow Yorkshireman, Richardson continued to reproach himself, crying, 'I can never forgive myself, never!'

Alfred Green, an Assemblies of God minister and family friend, offered to drive Wigglesworth to the funeral which was to commence at 2.45 p.m. (the Salters had gone on ahead as James was to conduct the service). As they traversed the snowbound Yorkshire countryside and drove through the towns and villages en route, Wigglesworth pointed out animatedly the churches and chapels where he and Polly had preached over the years. His companions that day – Green and his wife – remarked later that they had never seen him so jubilant and full of life.

In the vestry, the groans and the desperate prayers had ceased as it became clear that Smith Wigglesworth, who had raised many from the dead, was not going to rise himself. The four men lent forward to kiss his brow, rose from their knees, then stood with heads bowed, numbed by his sudden passing. The impasse was broken by a loud knock at the door. Wilfred Richardson's funeral cortège had arrived and the coffin, carried by Elder Hibbert's four sons, was gently lowered before the rostrum from which Richardson had so often preached.

James Salter emerged, ashen-faced from the vestry and walked solemnly to the pulpit to commence the service. Sitting in one of the front pews, Alice sensed there was something wrong. Her husband looked drawn and he seemed distant and detached as he announced the first hymn. She also wondered about the absence of her father. As the hymn drew to a close, Donald Gee also appeared and, after whispering a few words to Salter, replaced him in the pulpit, while the latter disappeared up the steps to the vestry. He reappeared as the final 'Amen' resounded throughout the church and beckoned to Alice to come forward. She rose quickly from the pew, suddenly apprehensive. As she studied her husband's worn face and as he quietly told her to go immediately to the vestry, she knew it was her father.

His voice trembling slightly, Salter at last revealed his secret: 'We now have a double sorrow,' he announced mournfully. 'One here,' pointing to the coffin, 'and one in there,' he said pointing to the vestry. The meaning was immediately obvious to the congregation: Smith Wigglesworth, whom they had seen enter not long before, had died. The sound of muffled gasps reverberated across the hall; some sobbed quietly while others sat motionless, their faces frozen in expressions of disbelief. In the vestry, Alice wept as she beheld the body of her father, but as the tears trickled down her cheeks, she smiled.

Smith Wigglesworth's sudden demise required James and Alice Salter to remain at the church and attend to the practical and legal formalities concerning an unexpected death, including an examination of the body by a physician. When the doctor arrived he duly examined Wigglesworth and then exclaimed in amazement, 'What a fine specimen of manhood! There is no visible cause of death. It is just like a workman coming home from his work, taking off his coat and settling down to rest.' Wigglesworth once declared to his wife that, 'No knife would ever touch this body, in life or in death.' And that prophecy came to pass, for even though a post mortem was prescribed by law to determine the cause of death, none was performed on his body.

Meanwhile, Donald Gee left with the other mourners to conduct a necessarily brief burial service for Richardson, while a snowstorm raged, before returning shivering with the rest of the funeral party to Glad Tidings Hall where refreshments were waiting. As they drank tea and sipped from bowls of piping hot soup, Gee slipped out unnoticed and quietly stole up the steps to the vestry for one last look at the dead evangelist. Gazing at Wigglesworth lying serene on the floor of the vestry, he recalled fondly with a wistful smile, the great Christian warrior's campaigns of the past: the thousands of souls saved; the multitudes healed of all manner of diseases; the legions of demons cast out; and, above all, his immense faith. Would there ever be another like him, he mused. As he turned to descend the steps to the chapel, it occurred to Gee that the unexpected events in Wakefield that day would soon send a ripple of shock and grief across the globe.

On 17 March, many of those who were present as Wilfred Richardson was laid to rest returned for Wigglesworth's funeral at Southend Hall, an Elim Four Square Gospel Church in Bradford. Donald Gee conducted the service, quoting from Hebrews 11, and again, the coffin was borne by Elder Hibbert's four sons. As the funeral party emerged from the church to the strains of the hymn, 'Have Faith in God, the Sun Will Shine', as if on cue, a shaft of sunlight broke through the dark, stormy clouds, bathing the coffin and its bearers in a golden hue.

The procession of almost two hundred and fifty mourners descended the valley from Southend Hall to the cemetery at Nabb Wood, Shipley, through deserted streets,[1] trailing in columns behind Wigglesworth's coffin and singing hymns as they went. At the graveside, Gee recited a selection of Wigglesworth's most beloved scriptures. Then, as the coffin was lowered gently into the grave, the mourners, many smiling bravely through their tears, sang the refrain that had resounded from pulpits and platforms around the world, 'Only believe, only believe, all things are possible, only believe . . .'

Smith Wigglesworth was laid to rest beside his beloved wife Polly and his son George. They would be joined in December 1964 by his daughter, Alice Salter. Inscribed on the granite headstone was the simple message that Wigglesworth had chosen himself thirty-four years before: 'I am the Resurrection and the Life.'

Albert Hibbert stood at the edge of the open grave gazing at Wigglesworth's coffin, the still calm of the cemetery, broken only by the monotonous drumming of earth on wood, as mourner after mourner scooped up a handful of frozen soil and hurled it onto the burnished black lid. Suddenly an anxious voice jolted Hibbert from his reverie: 'Albert, what are we going to do now?' Hibbert turned and stared at the man whose face was etched with fear and anguish, as though his faith were being buried with the dead patriarch. For a moment, he was lost for words. Then his jaw stiffened with resolve: 'I'm going on. What about you?' Turning to leave, Hibbert hunched his shoulders and tugged his collar higher, as a gust of icy wind sent a chill up his spine. Despite the bitter cold, he noticed that the sun was again peeking fitfully through the leaden clouds and snowdrops were piercing the thinning white mantle. Spring was coming at last.

Epilogue

THE WIGGLESWORTH LEGACY

More than sixty years have now elapsed since Smith Wigglesworth's death in March 1947 and he is, arguably, better known now than when he was alive. Numerous volumes of his sermons and teachings, as well as a number of accounts of his life have been published and the interest in Wigglesworth continues to grow.

Wigglesworth founded no movement, authored no books (although two were published in his name) had no official disciples, and no doctrine or theological college bears his name. He established but one church, whose final manifestation was the Bowland Street Mission, but when that ceased to exist as an independent entity in 1919, he remained unattached to any denomination or Christian body. Yet he stands, and rightly so, as a colossus in the Pentecostal movement, whose bold proclamation of Pentecost with signs following was instrumental in the development of the Pentecostal Church worldwide, particularly Elim and the Assemblies of God.

Through his audacious faith and spectacular healing ministry, Wigglesworth fanned the flames of revival in countries throughout the world. Thousands came to know Jesus Christ as their Saviour, received divine healing and were delivered from demonic oppression and possession as a result of his ministry, and these often formed the nucleus of newly-established Pentecostal assemblies. This was particularly evident in Switzerland, where it was noted that nine new Pentecostal churches were founded following his campaign in the country in 1920. And in New Zealand, Wigglesworth's two evangelistic campaigns there in 1922 and 1923–4 were credited as providing the impetus for the establishment of what was to become the Pentecostal Church of New Zealand.

But if Smith Wigglesworth, the plumber turned evangelist, has a lasting legacy then it is, perhaps, as an inspiration to generations of Christian men and women since his passing to take God at His Word and dare to believe that through faith, all things are indeed possible. Only heaven, surely, will reveal the full extent of the impact on humanity of his extraordinary life and ministry.

ENDNOTES

CHAPTER 1

1 Stanley Frodsham, *Smith Wigglesworth, Apostle of Faith* (Missouri: Gospel Publishing House, 1993), p.11. Used by permission.
2 Salvation Army, *The War Cry* (August 1880).

CHAPTER 2

1 Stanley Frodsham, *Smith Wigglesworth, Apostle of Faith* (Missouri: Gospel Publishing House, 1993), p.18. Used by permission.
2 Members of the Salvation Army were prohibited from marrying outside of the movement.

CHAPTER 3

1 Stanley Frodsham, *Smith Wigglesworth, Apostle of Faith* (Missouri: Gospel Publishing House, 1993), p.22. Used by permission.
2 Established in 1900 by John Alexander Dowie and located north of Chicago on Lake Michigan, Zion City grew to

approximately six thousand people during the following few years.

3 John Alexander Dowie (1847–1907) founder of Zion City. A controversial figure and advocate of divine healing, Dowie became increasingly eccentric in his latter years, becoming obsessed with eschatology and claiming to be the prophesied Elijah and first apostle of a renewed end-times church. In 1905, Dowie suffered a stroke while preparing to establish other Zions, and died disgraced and ignored two years later.

4 Some Pentecostal groups, including Zion City, believed that a convert should be immersed in water three times – once for each member of the Trinity.

5 An extension of the Holiness Movement, the non-denominational Keswick Convention was first held in 1875 in the town of Keswick in the Lake District, Cumbria.

6 Stanley Frodsham, *Smith Wigglesworth, Apostle of Faith* (Missouri: Gospel Publishing House, 1993), p.36. Used by permission.

CHAPTER 4

1 Evan Roberts (1878–1951) was one of the leaders of Welsh Revival that took place in 1904–5, the birthplace of which was the Rhondda Valley in South Wales in which the town of Tonypandy is located.

2 This incident appears to contradict Wigglesworth's assertion that he had been completely sanctified. Perhaps one could say that his sanctification was an on-going process.

3 Stanley Frodsham, *Smith Wigglesworth, Apostle of Faith* (Missouri: Gospel Publishing House, 1993), p.51. Used by permission.

CHAPTER 5

[1] It is possible that all four of Smith Wigglesworth's sons served in the British Armed Forces during World War I.

[2] Donald Gee, *The Pentecostal Movement* (USA: Elim Publishing Company, 1941), p.209.

CHAPTER 6

[1] Harry V. Roberts, *New Zealand's Greatest Revivals* (New Zealand: The Pelorus Press, 1951), p.29–30. Out of print.

[2] George Stormont, *Wigglesworth: A Man Who Walked With God* (USA: Harrison House, 1989), p.28.

[3] Stanley Frodsham, *Smith Wigglesworth, Apostle of Faith* (Missouri: Gospel Publishing House, 1993), p.69–70. Used by permission.

[4] Ibid., p.133.

[5] Ibid., p.143–4.

CHAPTER 7

[1] There is no evidence to suggest that Wigglesworth ever attended a Baptist church. It was likely that he was referring here to his water baptism, which occurred in 1876.

CHAPTER 8

[1] *Dominion* newspaper, New Zealand: May 1922.

[2] Jack Hywel-Davies, *Baptised by Fire* (London: Hodder & Stoughton, 1987), p.91. Used by permission.

[3] George Stormont, *Wigglesworth: A Man Who Walked With God* (USA: Harrison House, 1989), p.21.

CHAPTER 9

1   *The Sun* newspaper, New Zealand: 1922.
2   J.E. Worsfold, *A History of the Charismatic Movements in New Zealand* (Julian Literature Trust, 1974), p.149.
3   *New Zealand Baptist*, New Zealand: 1923.
4   There is no record of Wigglesworth being a member of, or being involved in, any committees, despite invitations, following his resignation from the PMU. This may have been due to the incident involving the PMU and his forced resignation from its Ruling Council.

CHAPTER 10

1   Curiously, Wigglesworth made this remark while preaching: 'Many years ago, God healed me when all my teeth were decayed and weak. God healed them when I was sixty-two [in 1921].' This seems to contradict the episode involving Dr Lanz.
2   Stanley Frodsham, *Smith Wigglesworth, Apostle of Faith* (Missouri: Gospel Publishing House, 1993), p.105. Used by permission.
3   Harry V. Roberts (1863–1949) was one of the founders of the Wellington City Mission, renamed the New Zealand Evangelical Mission, that became the Pentecostal Church of New Zealand in 1924, of which he was the first General Superintendent.
4   There is an unconfirmed report of a similar incident occurring in San Francisco. One writer claims that people in the city were healed as Wigglesworth walked through the streets and his shadow touched them.
5   Stanley Frodsham, *Smith Wigglesworth, Apostle of Faith* (Missouri: Gospel Publishing House, 1993), p.76–7. Used by permission.

6. *Dominion* newspaper, New Zealand: May 1922.

7. Harry V. Roberts, *New Zealand's Greatest Revivals* (New Zealand: The Pelorus Press, 1951), p.19. Out of print.

8. Ibid., p.27.

9. *Marlborough Express*, Marlborough: December 1923.

10. Barry Chant, *Heart of Fire* (Luke Publications). Out of print.

11. Stanley Frodsham, *Smith Wigglesworth, Apostle of Faith* (Missouri: Gospel Publishing House, 1993), p.93–4. Used by permission.

CHAPTER 11

¹ Stanley Frodsham, *Smith Wigglesworth, Apostle of Faith* (Missouri: Gospel Publishing House, 1993), p.139. Used by permission.

² This must have come as a surprise to Wigglesworth himself, as he had, on more than one occasion, warned against the influence of the Roman Catholic Church, declaring while preaching in 1924: 'You take care it [the Roman Catholic Church] does not rise again, the Roman power is always bloodshed and murder and always against the Holy Spirit . . . '

³ David du Plessis, *A Man Called Mr Pentecost* (New Jersey: Bridge-Logos Publishing, 1977) p.2–3. Used by permission.

CHAPTER 12

¹ Seth Wigglesworth's wife, Florence, had a sister whose husband was Assistant Chief Constable of Bradford. He was able to arrange for the roads leading to the cemetery to be kept clear for the funeral.

BIBLIOGRAPHY

Chant, Barry, *Heart of Fire* (Luke Publications). Out of print.

Donald Gee Centre for Pentecostal and Charismatic Research. Material used by permission.

du Plessis, David, *A Man Called Mr Pentecost* (New Jersey: Bridge-Logos, 1977). Used by permission.

Frodsham, Stanley, *Smith Wigglesworth, Apostle of Faith* (Missouri: Gospel Publishing House, 1993). Used by permission.

Gee, Donald, *The Pentecostal Movement* (USA: Elim Publishing, 1941).

Hacking, William, *A Life Ablaze With the Power of God* (USA: Harrison House, 1995).

Hibbert, Albert, *Smith Wigglesworth: The Secret of His Power* (USA: Harrison House, 1982).

Hywel-Davies, Jack, *Baptised by Fire* (London: Hodder & Stoughton, 1987). Used by permission.

Roberts, Harry V., *New Zealand's Greatest Revival* (New Zealand: Pelorus Press, 1951). Out of print.

Stormont, George, *Wigglesworth: A Man Who Walked With God* (USA: Harrison House, 1989).

Salvation Army, *The War Cry* (August 1880).

Worsfold, J. E., *A History of the Charismatic Movements in New Zealand* (Julian Literature Trust, 1974).

The Wesleys

*Two Men Who
Changed the World*

Julian Wilson

ohn and Charles Wesley are among the most influential Christians who
have ever lived. The Methodist movement they founded changed the
face of eighteenth-century England, in an age that was rife with cor-
ruption, crime and religious apathy. Over more than five decades, John
Wesley travelled ceaselessly on horseback, preaching gospel sermons that
transformed whole communities. Charles Wesley became probably the
most prolific hymn writer in history, his works still favourites in many
congregations to this day.

n this comprehensive dual biography, best-selling author Julian Wilson
provides a detailed account of the Wesley brothers' lives and ministries,
including their conversion experiences, their triumphs and failures, their
relationships with women, their prison outreach, their writings and
preaching, and, in John's case, supernatural ministry, involvement in the
abolition of slavery, and educational and social welfare initiatives.

978-1-78078-119-8

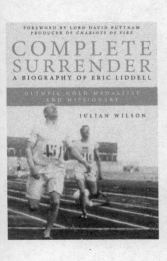

Complete Surrender

A Biography of Eric Liddell
Olympic Gold Medallist and Missionary

Julian Wilson

'On a stiflingly hot Parisian afternoon in July 1924, six athletes lined up for the start of the Olympic 400 metres. In the sixth and outside lane was the Scottish sprint sensation Eric Liddell . . .'

Liddell made headlines by refusing to race on a Sunday. His switch from 100 metres to 400 metres, and subsequent triumph, is now legendary.

Liddell brought the same singleness of purpose to his faith as to his running. This vivid biography recounts his career as a missionary in war-torn China, his unassuming and selfless character, and his delight in practical jokes. It includes interviews with his family and friends, extracts from his letters and a number of rare photographs.

978-1-86024-841-2

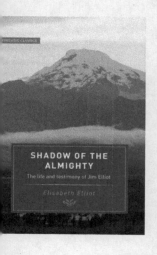

Shadow of the Almighty

*The Life and Testimony
of Jim Elliot*

Elisabeth Elliot

'He is no fool who gives what he cannot keep to gain what he cannot ~~lose.~~'

~~F~~ew books have had such a great impact as this life and testament of Jim ~~E~~lliot written by his wife, Elisabeth. He was a man of passion and a man ~~o~~f prayer, an earthly man with a heavenly mind, whose story continues ~~to~~ inspire today.

~~S~~hadow of the Almighty chronicles his journey from childhood in ~~O~~regon and his college days at Wheaton to the mission fields of Ecua~~d~~or where he eventually gave his life, aged 28. Full of journal excerpts ~~an~~d personal letters, we are introduced to this great man, his struggles, ~~hi~~s ambitions, his loves, his dreams and his all-consuming passion for ~~C~~hrist and his kingdom. This book will challenge you to give your life ~~w~~holeheartedly to Christ.

978-1-85078-625-2

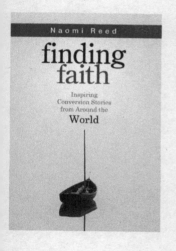

Finding Faith

*Inspiring Conversion Stories
from Around the World*

Naomi Reed

'We will have no more Voodoo in our house. It's true that the Voodoo has power, but the One I believe in has much more power. And because of his power, the Voodoo can't hurt you, or any of us, anymore' (Alberic, Benin).

A collection of inspirational stories from around the world, sharing the exciting and life-changing transformation that Jesus brings. From the flat, dry towns of Uganda to northern Iraq, from the land of the native Australians to the former Soviet Union, Naomi Reed shares moving accounts of ordinary people who have put their faith in the Lord Jesus Christ. They all say the same thing . . . God's love is amazing, and it changes everything.

978-1-78078-462-5

Authentic

We trust you enjoyed reading this book from Authentic. If you want to be informed of any new titles from this author and other releases you can sign up to the Authentic newsletter by scanning below:

Online:
authenticmedia.co.uk

Follow us: